CANADA'S ATLANTIC GATEWAY

AN ILLUSTRATED HISTORY OF THE PORT OF HALIFAX

JAMES D. FROST

For my parents

Copyright © James D. Frost 2008

All rights reserved. No part of this book may be reproduced, stored in a retrieval system or transmitted in any form or by any means without the prior written permission from the publisher, or, in the case of photocopying or other reprographic copying, permission from Access Copyright, 1 Yonge Street, Suite 1900, Toronto, Ontario, M5E 1E5.

Nimbus Publishing Limited, PO Box 9166, Halifax, NS, B3K 5M8
(902) 455-4286, www.nimbus.ca

Printed and bound in Canada
Design: John van der Woude; Author photo: Precision Photographic Services Ltd.

Library and Archives Canada Cataloguing in Publication

    Frost, James Douglas, 1953-
    Canada's Atlantic gateway : an illustrated history of the Port of
    Halifax / James Frost.
    Includes index.
    ISBN 978-1-55109-678-0 (hardcover edition ISBN 978-155109-698-8)
1. Halifax Harbour (N.S.)—History. I. Title.
HE554.H34F76 2008   971.6'225   C2008-904051-1

We acknowledge the financial support of the Government of Canada through the Book Publishing Industry Development Program (BPIDP) and the Canada Council, and of the Province of Nova Scotia through the Department of Tourism, Culture and Heritage for our publishing activities.

Table of Contents

Map of the Port of Halifax VI

Foreword VII

Acknowledgements IX

Introduction 1

ONE The Founding of Halifax, 1749–1815 7

TWO Building the Entrepôt, 1816–1866 17

THREE The Wharf of the Dominion, 1867–1913 45

FOUR The Great War, 1914–1918 77

FIVE The Open Gateway, 1919–1938 91

SIX Halifax and the Battle of the Atlantic, 1939–1945 119

SEVEN The Winter Port, 1946–1970 135

EIGHT The Container Age, 1971–1998 165

NINE Canada's Atlantic Gateway, 1999–2008 191

APPENDIX Halifax Port Administration 213

Notes 217

Image Sources 224

Index 225

Foreword

In 1749, a day after arriving in Halifax, Edward Cornwallis wrote, "All the officers agree, the harbour is the finest they have ever seen."[1] As true today as the day the words were uttered many years ago, this is the story of a very special place in the world, a place that has been endowed with "a generous gift of nature," a place where ships and people from many nations have sought safe haven from the earliest times, a place that has been a gateway to Canada even before there was a Canada.

The story begins simply enough. Once upon a time, there was great harbour on the edge of the Atlantic Ocean, a gateway to a new land. Early explorers and mariners marvelled at this port, which had all the natural attributes they needed—it was deep, ice-free year-round, sheltered, and strategically located. And when the new country began to develop, railways were built to span the distance from this fine port to the main centres of commerce. Over the years, this gateway diligently served the social, commercial, and military needs of the country, giving much and asking little in return. Carrying on through storms, wars, and disasters, the wharves, piers, and cargo sheds were built and added to when funds allowed. The number of ships, cargoes, and passengers has ebbed and flowed over the years, yet all the while the port has moved steadily forward. The port has been both favoured and challenged by modern industry and technology. Where opportunity presented, port administrators latched on, leading to new developments that enabled the gateway to open more widely to the world.

It has been said that "History is a guide to navigation in perilous times. History is who we are and why we are the way we are."[2] So too, is our history—the stories of the diligent, industrious, smart, strategic, far-sighted, aware, well-equipped, stalwart, brave, loyal, and committed people of the Port of Halifax, Canada's Atlantic Gateway, yesterday and today. With determination as our compass and history as our guide, we continue to navigate through perilous times.

We hope you will find this book as fascinating and thought-provoking as we have during our research and writing. History is, indeed, a great teacher, and we have learned many lessons for the future, and much about ourselves. A sincere thank you to everyone who contributed to the work during production, and primarily for the fine research and writing skills of author James Frost and to the endless hours of painstaking archival work by Lorraine Brenton, Steve Patterson, Glen Hicks, and Robert Todd.

Karen Oldfield
President and CEO
Halifax Port Authority

Acknowledgements

This has been a dream assignment for me in every respect. It appeals to me as a historian of Maritime-region business, but also as someone who has spent most of his career in and around the shipping industry. I have often wondered how a kid from the suburbs of Montreal, who studied history at McGill, could end up working in the shipping industry and writing a history of the Port of Halifax. My involvement with the port is owed largely to the man who first hired me, Gary Blaikie. Gary took a chance on a very green graduate with an MA in history and hired me as a business analyst at the former Halifax-Dartmouth Port Commission. Shipping and ports have been one of my great passions ever since.

I would like to take the opportunity to thank the port's History Project steering committee, led by the indefatigable Lorraine Brenton, for having the inspiration to pursue such a project in the first place, and for providing me with the guidance and support to complete it. I would also like to thank the port's president and CEO, Karen Oldfield, for bringing me "into the tent" and inviting me to pursue this project.

In the course of completing the project, the port lost four very important personalities who helped shape the modern Port of Halifax. Bill Mingo was chairman of the Halifax-Dartmouth Port Commission when I was hired in 1980, F. H. "Joe" Howard was the first president of Halterm, Victor Bayne was executive director of the commission and my boss from 1983 to 1987, and Ray Beck was a long-serving employee of the National Harbours Board in Halifax, retiring as general manager of the Halifax Port Corporation in 1985. I also lost a dear friend and mentor, Bill March, whose friendship I cherished from the day I moved to Halifax in 1975. Sadly, my own mother, Dorothy Frost, passed away in May 2008, as this manuscript was being finalized.

Last, but not least, I would like to thank my wife, Jane Grantmyre, and our son, David, for putting up with (actually *without*) me while I went through the contortions of writing this book.

Introduction

The Port of Halifax has been renowned for generations and its growth and development is part of every Haligonian's birthright. At some point, all schoolchilden in Nova Scotia learn that Halifax Harbour is the second-largest natural harbour in the world, surpassed only by Sydney, Australia.

The port's fortunes have ebbed and flowed along with the development of the surrounding city. The port flourished during times of war, including the War of 1812, the U.S. Civil War, and both world wars. It was a major North Atlantic entrepôt during the Age of Sail, from which ships carried goods and people to the four corners of the world and established strong trading links with Britain, the "Boston states," and the West Indies. It was integral to Canada's immigration strategies in the mid-twentieth century, acting as a gateway for people entering the country. It is now a busy container port, welcoming ships from around the world and distributing their goods to the rest of the country.

Halifax Harbour looking south from Bedford Basin

During the port's early days in the nineteenth century, three rival transportation systems—the Intercolonial Railway (ICR), the Canadian Pacific Railway (CPR), and the Grand Trunk Railway (GTR)—served the ports of Halifax; Saint John; and Portland, Maine; respectively. At the turn of the century, Portland had, in effect, become Canada's winter port, much to the chagrin of local promoters, who felt that Confederation should benefit Canadian ports, not American ones. One of the promises that Upper Canada had made to Maritime interests prior to Confederation was that Halifax and Saint John would become Canada's wintertime outlets for trade and commerce, as the St. Lawrence River was unnavigable during its winter freeze, making Montreal, the main entrepôt for goods entering Upper Canada, inaccessible. But the Upper Canadians argued that the American route was shorter, faster, and therefore less expensive. It did not seem to matter to them that the ICR had been built along New Brunswick's north shore for military and political reasons, and not for economic ones. The ICR's longer and more circuitous route via eastern New Brunswick rather than a "short line" directly through western New Brunswick as its surveyor Sandford Fleming had preferred was always held against Halifax and its port boosters.

As is still evident to any visitor of Halifax, the city grew up around its original finger piers, which were located downtown, adjacent to the wharves owned by its merchants and shipowners. These finger piers were an essential characterizing feature of downtown Halifax. As vessels became larger, they required larger amounts of backup land and shed space, which could not be provided at the existing finger piers. Nor could Halifax's aspirations to become Canada's winter port be adequately served from the downtown finger piers. As a result, port activity moved north to Richmond Terminals and Deep Water Terminals.

OPPOSITE
A Halifax finger pier belonging to A&M Smith Company, circa 1940

With the outbreak of war in 1914, the role of Canadian ports, including Halifax, took on new importance. Port activities now included ferrying goods, supplies, and soldiers to the front in Europe. The Port of Halifax certainly proved its worth during the war. Indeed, in 1918 the London *Times* called Halifax the "third most important port in the World."[1] However, the war also brought the traumatic events of the Halifax Explosion, which destroyed much of the port's infrastructure.

Following the devastation wreaked upon Richmond Terminals by the explosion, pre-war plans were revived to develop an enormous terminal site in the south end of the city, immediately adjacent to the harbour's entrance. The new site, Ocean Terminals, was developed over a seven-year period from 1921 to 1928. Stone from a massive railway cut was used for landfill, and the neighbourhood was transformed from a mainly pastoral setting with large estates into a busy port and industrial area. With the new terminals came the development of a grain elevator and cold storage facility. Later, Ocean Terminals expanded to include Piers 26 to 28, as well as Pier B. With its deep water, Ocean Terminals could handle the largest vessels afloat. In fact, the berthing water was, according to historian Thomas Raddall, "deeper than is required by any vessel now afloat or planned."[2] Three vessels could be accommodated at once, and the facilities included "the finest passenger traffic accommodation on the Western Atlantic coast." Pier 21 became "The Gateway to Canada," and hundreds of thousands of immigrants entered the country through its doors.

With the opening of the St. Lawrence Seaway in 1956, ports from Montreal all the way to the westernmost extremity of Lake Superior were opened to ocean-going vessels, and Halifax was once again relegated to the status of a winter port. After playing an important role year-round during the Second World War, promoters of the Port of Halifax were no longer satisfied with just being a winter port.

Despite the new competition from ports along the St. Lawrence Seaway, the total tonnage handled in Halifax remained static after the war. When icebreaking commenced on the St. Lawrence River in 1966, making the Port of Montreal accessible year-round, Halifax's base of activity was further threatened.

The next big change took place in 1970, with the development of Pier C and the construction of the Halterm Container Terminal adjacent to Point Pleasant Park. There are many reasons given by many different people as to why this site was chosen, but it appears to have simply been the path of least resistance, the quickest way to get to Halifax on the container map, so to speak. Halterm, the first "common user" container terminal in Canada, was built by a consortium of Canadian National, Clarke Transportation Canada Ltd., and Halicon, which was a Crown corporation owned eighty percent by the Province of Nova Scotia and twenty percent by the City of Halifax. A year earlier, Manchester Liners had opened the first container terminal in the country in Montreal, but the terminal was only for its own private use. Halifax's concept, however, was based on the idea that its container terminal would be available for any shipping line that could be attracted to the Port of Halifax. The Department of Transport in Ottawa approved Halifax's proposal in December 1968, and Halterm Ltd. opened for business in November 1970. Halifax built on this base until the early 1980s, handling over 200,000 TEUs (twenty-foot equivalent units) annually, and ranking in the top five North American East Coast ports, and the top thirty worldwide.

An aerial view of Halifax showing Point Pleasant Park and the Halterm Container Terminal

The port lost a significant portion of its business in 1981, when Dart Containerline decided to move its operations to Montreal. But despite this massive setback, developments in the container industry appeared to be working in Halifax's favour. The trends toward "Generation

The container terminal at Fairview Cove

III" vessels of over 3,000 TEU capacity, round-the-world services, and the establishment of load-centre ports (ports at which a large amount of hinterland cargo and transhipment cargo would be handled) all benefited the Port of Halifax greatly, and a second container terminal was opened at Fairview Cove in 1982. By the end of the decade, Halifax could boast that it had attracted over twenty-five shipping lines moving almost 450,000 TEUs through the port annually.

In 2008, new developments are taking place along the old seawall, with the arrival of the Nova Scotia College of Art and Design (NSCAD) University Port Campus, the expansion of Pier 21 into Canada's Immigration Museum, the construction of a new farmers' market, and the opening of the Cunard Centre home-port facility and special events centre. On the cargo side, Consolidated FastFrate opened a new 90,000 square foot (8,400 square metre) transload facility in Burnside Industrial Park, which, along with other such facilities, is expected to evolve into a gateway logistics park. The port has also launched a major initiative to develop the Indian subcontinent market, where it has a substantial advantage in time and distance over competing ports, using a Suez routing. In 2006, the first regular calls by post-Panamax vessels (vessels too wide and too long to pass through the Panama Canal) commenced at the port, and a major new investor, Macquarie Infrastructure Partners, purchased the Halterm container facility for over $170 million. While the Port of Halifax is currently facing several short-term challenges, the future looks bright, indeed.

CHAPTER ONE

The Founding of Halifax
1749–1815

Halifax, or *Chebucto*, was occupied long before the Europeans "officially" arrived in 1749. The Mi'kmaq had been there for eleven thousand years, since the Ice Age. In the early days, they came for hunting and fishing in the summer, then retreated to the Minas Basin and Bay of Fundy in the winter. The great harbour saw no other visitors until European fishing and exploration expeditions began arriving in the fifteenth century.

Samuel de Champlain visited the harbour in 1607 upon his departure from Acadia. He explored the coast between LaHave and Canso in a shallop, or small reconnaissance craft, observing and mapping Mahone and St. Margaret's bays, Sambro, Chebucto Bay (Halifax), Jeddore, Country Harbour, and St. Mary's River. Champlain referred to Chebucto as "*une baie fort saine,*" or a "good safe bay."[1] Almost a century after Champlain's explorations, Jacques-Francois de Monbeton de Brouillan, the commandant of *Placentia* and *Acadia*, put into Chebucto in the

A conceptual engraving of Samuel de Champlain by Théophile Hamel, circa 1866

spring of 1701 on his way to Port Royal. As Thomas Raddall recounts in *Warden of the North*, Brouillan wrote, "The port is one of the finest nature could form."[2] The harbour continued to be used as a safe haven for French explorers, as well as fishermen from New England, throughout the eighteenth century.

In 1713, the Treaty of Utrecht ceded mainland Nova Scotia to the British, and the French concentrated their efforts on protecting the entrance to the St. Lawrence with the construction of the Fortress of Louisbourg, which they built between 1719 and 1745. Louisbourg fell to the British in 1745, but a year later the inexperienced lieutenant general of the French naval forces, Duc d'Anville, sailed for Nova Scotia with a fleet of between fifty-four and seventy-one vessels and as many as eleven thousand soldiers and sailors (these figures vary depending on the source) determined to recapture the fort.[3] The fleet was to rendezvous with a French squadron from the West Indies at Chebucto, from whence they were to lay siege in an attempt to recapture Louisbourg. However, the expedition was aborted after d'Anville died of apoplexy. The Treaty of Aix-la-Chappelle, which ended the War of the Austrian Succession, finally returned Louisbourg to the French in 1748. This lent some urgency to the establishment of a permanent British settlement in what was still a largely French-speaking colony.

EARLY SETTLEMENT

The founding of Halifax as a permanent European settlement was led by Edward Cornwallis in late June 1749. Halifax was meant to be a British counterpoint to the great fortress at Louisbourg, which was once again in French hands. Cornwallis led an expedition of some twenty-five hundred soldiers and settlers sailing from the River Thames. A day after Cornwallis arrived at Chebucto, he wrote, "All the officers agree, it is the finest harbour they have ever seen."[4] In mid-summer, the fledgling settlement was renamed Halifax, after George Dunk, Lord Halifax.

Early on, Halifax was a British colonial outpost, dominated by the military. But its location on the North Atlantic, sandwiched between the colonial empires of Britain and France, and within comparatively easy sailing distances from the American colonies and the West Indies, afforded many opportunities for trade and commerce. In February 1750, it was proposed in the provincial Legislative Council to build a quay along the shore in front of the town, but several merchants, including Joshua Mauger, who had purchased water lots, thought the project too expensive and time-consuming. Instead, the merchants were given licences to build their own wharves.

Mauger, one of the colony's first shipowners and merchants, was a Jersey sea captain and politician who developed a wide array of economic interests during his eleven years in Halifax.[5] Many of those pursuits, like his continued trade with Louisbourg, brought him into conflict with local authorities. His lands were extensive, and he owned twenty-thousand-acre estates in both Cumberland County and St. John's Island (present-day Prince Edward Island). He also owned the largest fleet of ships in Halifax in this period, with twenty-seven vessels. Mauger's ships engaged in a pattern of trade that was to endure for many generations: fish and lumber to the West Indies; rum, molasses, and sugar in return. His ships also carried rum around the coast to stores in Annapolis Royal, Minas, and Chignecto, and imported a variety of manufactured goods and foodstuffs from Great Britain.

TOP
Colonel Edward Cornwallis

BOTTOM
Joshua Mauger

DEVELOPING TRADE LINKAGES

By 1780, two large vessels, *Adamant* and *St. Lawrence*, provided regular service between Halifax and Great Britain. Likewise, Halifax developed trade linkages with the West Indies, especially in the wake of the American Revolution, which ended in 1783. With American ports no longer part of the British Empire, Halifax's trade with the Caribbean colonies soared. Even minor ship-owners were sending cargoes of fish, hogsheads (barrels), salmon, shingles, lumber, and cod liver oil to the Caribbean in exchange for rum and molasses. In 1787, a number of merchants formed the Halifax Marine Association to promote the town's trade.

Throughout this period, Halifax's port infrastructure was steadily evolving. In 1796, the first of many proposals to build a bridge across the narrows was presented to the House of Assembly. A few years later, in 1799, a hurricane partially destroyed Market Wharf and King's Wharf, while the Market Slip was destroyed completely. The total loss of property and shipping was estimated at £100,000. In 1800, a new market was built in an open space opposite King's Wharf. At the same time, public monies were expended on repairing the Market Slip and constructing a fish market.

By the early nineteenth century, the population of Halifax had grown to 8,532, with about 1,000 dwellings. Settlement was concentrated around the foot of George Street; it began to spread out towards the south and west, but was still largely hemmed in by the Citadel, the construction of which had been started by the British garrison in 1758. Even though development was sporadic, the town began to evolve beyond just a military garrison and was becoming a dynamic centre of trade, although the Napoleonic Wars would continue to emphasize the town's role as a naval stronghold.

OPPOSITE
Richard Short, a purser in the Royal Navy, sketched this scene depicting the town and harbour of Halifax in 1759.

The Napoleonic Wars raged on and off from 1793 to 1815. The port's trade levels dropped considerably in 1804 due to the number of captures by enemy privateers and the undercutting of fish prices in the Caribbean by U.S. competitors.[6] The Peace of Amiens had put a temporary halt to European hostilities between 1802 and 1803, but Nova Scotia's privateers were active once again after hostilities resumed in 1804.

The United States attempted to remain neutral throughout the war, but placed an embargo on British trade in 1807. Britain responded by declaring Halifax, Shelburne, Saint John, and St. Andrews to be "free" ports that undermined the embargo. New England merchants took advantage by selling their own cargoes and purchasing manufactured goods in these free ports. Meanwhile, Halifax merchants shipped cargoes to markets in the West Indies in convoys protected by British naval escorts.

OPPOSITE
An engraving by Lt. Col. Edward Hicks depicting the settlement of Halifax (looking north from Point Pleasant to Citadel Hill), circa 1780

THE WAR OF 1812

The War of 1812, fought between Britain and the United States from June 1812 to the spring of 1815, had an enormous impact on Halifax and the rest of the colony.[7] Revenue receipts for the Port of Halifax tripled from £31,000 in 1812 to over £93,000 in 1814, before dropping to a little over £60,000 in 1815 after the war ended. During the war, Halifax emerged as an entrepôt between Britain and New England, which refused to engage in the conflict. Halifax was the scene of much rejoicing when, in June 1813, HMS *Shannon* arrived in port with the USS *Chesapeake* in tow, following a brief skirmish off Boston Harbor.

Numerous fortunes were made privateering during the war, and approximately forty vessels were outfitted for this purpose. The most famous privateer, and undoubtedly the most

RIGHT
Letter of Marque and seal issued to Caleb Seely, commander of the privateer ship *Liverpool Packet*, November 19, 1813

FAR RIGHT
One of a four-part lithograph series produced by J. G. Schetly portraying the capture of USS *Chesapeake* by HMS *Shannon* during the War of 1812

14 CANADA'S ATLANTIC GATEWAY

Enos Collins (1774–1871), circa 1870

successful, was Enos Collins, who began to amass his fortune during the War of 1812 with his ownership of the dreaded *Liverpool Packet*. Through privateering, astute wartime trading, and investing, Collins eventually established himself as the richest man in Canada.

The war period was a raucous time in Halifax. The area of present-day Brunswick Street in front of the town clock was called "Knock Him Down Row" due to the frequent fights outside of the brothels and barracks in the area. Halifax's merchants had concentrated on making the town a linchpin between the United States and Britain, and the resulting activity had "swept away the contents of [the] stores and shops like a torrent."[8] According to Brian Cuthbertson, the streets of Halifax were said to be paved with gold during this time.[9] But after the war ended, peacetime brought with it vastly reduced military spending, dropping from £56,000 annually in 1812–15 to £25,000 in 1816–19, and Halifax's era of prosperity would soon come to an end.[10]

CHAPTER TWO

Building the Entrepôt
1816–1866

As Halifax has found many times in its history, the post-war period was difficult. The early 1820s were a time of profound readjustment for the city. The merchants of Halifax lobbied London for the type of protection that would recreate the boom-time conditions of the previous decade, but Halifax suffered from being outside the main commercial battleground between the U.S. and England as the two countries now struggled for trade supremacy in North America.

By the summer of 1822, commercial activity in Halifax was at a virtual standstill. Meanwhile, a strong timber trade made Saint John, New Brunswick, a formidable rival, and it eclipsed Halifax in both population and overall importance. Economic conditions began to improve after 1822, resulting from a new direction in imperial policy and the gradual abandonment of mercantilism, which had required that colonial trade be confined to the "mother" country. The "Great Reforms" of William Huskisson, the president of the Imperial Board of Trade in

Saint John, New Brunswick, pictured here in the late 1800s, played a more strategic mercantile role than Halifax during the early years of the nineteenth century.

London, resulted in a restructuring of the British Navigation Acts in 1825. Responding to concerns of the Halifax business community, he announced that, except for certain commodities such as sugar, rum, and salt fish, "there was to be free intercourse between British colonies and reciprocating countries, either in British ships or ships of those countries." A wide range of manufactures and raw materials of foreign origin would be admitted into the colonies under very low tariff rates. Furthermore, as historian David Sutherland writes, bonded warehouse facilities were to be established at key colonial ports, such as Halifax, "with the purpose of making them entrepôts in the trade between Europe and the states of South America."[1]

The changes to the Navigation Acts, which brought a degree of protection for colonial merchants, were short-lived. In 1830, Halifax's merchant community was concerned by a decision to adopt a policy of free trade, which, amongst other implications, would open the West Indies to American shipping, thereby threatening the prosperity of the North American colonies. The free-trade policy would allow American ships carrying U.S. goods to have access to ports in the British West Indies, while British and colonial ships would have comparable entry to American ports. Realizing the impact the new policy would have on the Maritime colonies, the British relented to some degree by applying duties to certain commodities when they were imported from another British colony.

Under the new rules, American produce could be imported duty-free and then re-exported to the West Indies as coming from a British colony, theoretically opening up the West Indies trade to both American and British shipping. In actual fact, American ships were not able to secure a large share of the trade. Nonetheless, between 1832 and 1833, the overall volume of Nova Scotia's imports declined substantially, from £1,454,973 to £1,035,660, while exports dropped from £914,841 to £887,367. By 1834, a full-blown recession had ensued; imports declined further, to just £853,987, while exports were a mere £755,005. Nova Scotia's exports to Great Britain and the rest of British North America had increased marginally, but were overwhelmed by a twenty-eight percent decline in exports to the British West Indies and a sixty-five percent decrease in exports to the U.S. Timber duties were lowered in the early 1840s, but were not slashed seriously until mid-decade. Repeal of the Corn Laws in 1846 and Britain's Navigation Acts of 1849 inflicted further damage on colonial shipping and lumber interests.[2]

THE HALIFAX FLEET

Halifax, as might be expected, was one of the major shipowning centres in the Atlantic region for much of the nineteenth century. It was also the main commercial and distribution centre for Nova Scotia.[3] Halifax merchants and shipowners participated in four major trades: with Britain, with the U.S. East Coast, with the West Indies, and the coasting trade. As the century progressed, Halifax owners began investing in medium-sized square-riggers, and by the 1860s and 70s, large square-riggers were employed in the deep-sea trades. In total number of vessels, the Halifax fleet was very large, second in the region only to St. John's, Newfoundland.

Square-riggers lined up along the Halifax waterfront, circa 1900

In total tonnage, it was second to Saint John, New Brunswick, whose merchants tended to build larger vessels from the outset. Over seventy percent of the Halifax fleet was under one hundred tons in capacity, and in the class above five hundred tons it represented only three percent of registrations. This changed dramatically in the 1860s and 70s, when the city's owners registered 208 vessels of five hundred tons or more. Overall, Halifax "developed a large coastal and fishing fleet...and a large fleet of medium-sized brigs, barques and ships," reflecting the city's role as a regional entrepôt.[4]

The Halifax Packet Company, or Halifax and Liverpool Trading Company, was organized in May 1825 to run the first non-government packet service between Nova Scotia and England. The idea behind it was to trade fish products for manufactured goods, while also transporting passengers between the two countries. The 331-ton *Atlantic* was built for this purpose in 1826 for partners James Bain, Lawrence Hartshorne, James N. Shannon, James McNab, and William Stairs. Another of their vessels was *Halifax*, a ship-rigged vessel of 344 tons. The same partners, along with Andrew Russel and William Foster, built and owned *Corsair* from 1826 to 1841. In his diary, William Stairs, a ship chandler and general merchant, mentions *Corsair* landing in Halifax in April 1828 and sailing for Liverpool on December 24. *Corsair* made the trip from Halifax to Liverpool in March–April 1830 in only twenty days, and was one of the company's most reliable assets, carrying mainly lumber.[5]

EXPANDING THE HINTERLAND

A persistent problem for Halifax was the lack of transportation links to other population centres in the region. As early as 1794 there was recognition of the need for a better transportation network. Lieutenant-Governor Sir John Wentworth recommended a canal system from Halifax to Truro using the traditional Mi'kmaq canoe route through the Dartmouth lakes. Because their port did not possess a natural hinterland, the merchants of Halifax attempted to extend their influence over much of the province by building the Shubenacadie Canal, a waterway running from Dartmouth on the eastern side of the province to Maitland on the Bay of Fundy. The Shubenacadie Canal Co. was incorporated in 1818 to complete this project. Its largest shareholders comprised the elite of Halifax: Samuel Cunard and Thomas Jeffrey, with forty shares

Sir John Wentworth, Lieutenant-Governor of Nova Scotia from 1792 to 1808

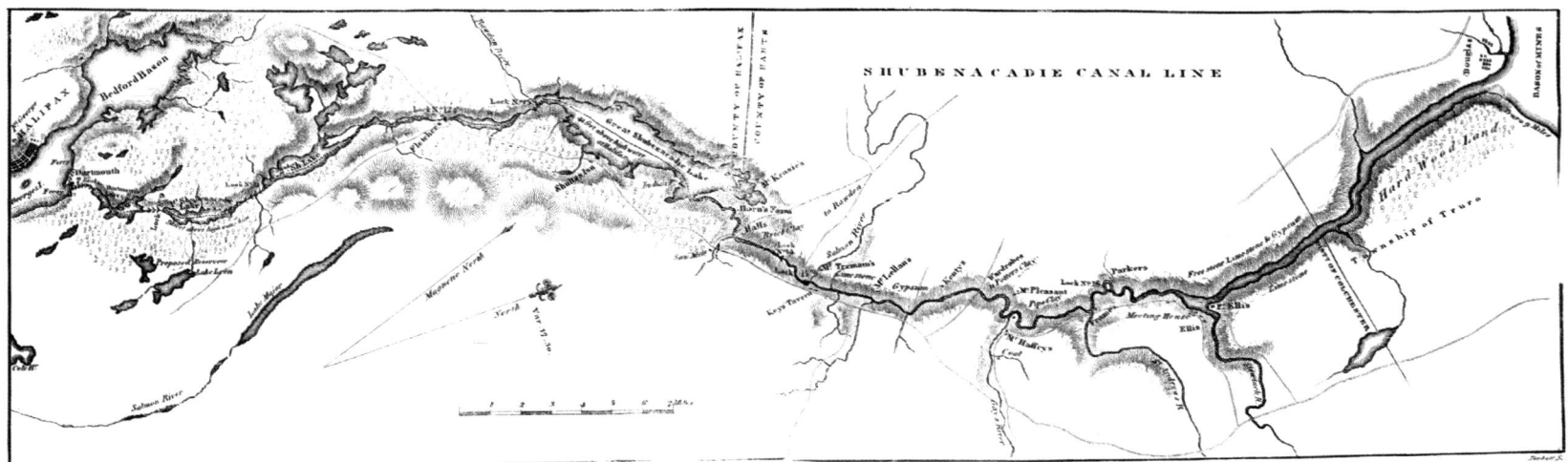

An early map showing the optimistic plans for the Shubenacadie Canal

each; Sir James Kempt, with twenty shares; Joseph Allison and John and Michael Tobin, with ten each; Charles Fairbanks, with eight; and three individuals, including William Stairs, with four shares each.[6]

Construction on the Shubenacadie Canal began in 1826 with the Earl of Dalhousie turning the sod. In 1827, the vessel *Corsair* was chartered to bring skilled stonecutters and masons from Scotland to aid in the construction of the canal. The directors of the Shubenacadie Canal Co. sent a memorandum to Lieutenant-Governor Sir Peregrine Maitland in 1829, petitioning the British Parliament to support the canal's construction. They had already received a modest grant of £15,000 from the Nova Scotia Legislature, and the initial subscription money of £60,000 was almost paid up. But, according to the petitioners, there was "not enough capital in such a young colony" to fund the project entirely. They claimed the canal would make the valuable resources of the province's interior easier to bring to world markets. There was also a defence argument: in the War of 1812, the only line of communication between Halifax and Saint John had been the long and hazardous voyage around the province and into the Bay of Fundy. The canal would solve this problem by providing a safe inland route between the two

South-facing view of Halifax Harbour from Crichton Manor in Dartmouth, circa 1870. The circular body of water in the centre of the photo is Sullivan's Pond, a man-made section of the Shubenacadie Canal.

cities. Completion of the whole canal and building of the requisite steamboats was estimated to cost an additional £50,000 over and above the initial subscription. The directors implored Westminster to look to the precedent set in Upper Canada, where the British government had assisted in the construction of both the Rideau and Welland canals. They were hoping to have the work completed within two years, and offered free passage to government troops and agents. Their plea succeeded to some extent, and they were loaned £20,000 for ten years.

When the canal was almost complete in 1831, Nova Scotia's notorious freeze and thaw cycles wreaked considerable damage on a dam that had been built at the northern end of Lake Charles. The Royal Engineers estimated that £127,000 in damage had been done; the company secretary, Charles Fairbanks, had a different estimate, which suggested it would cost almost £500,000 to repair. The canal was abandoned in 1831 when the investors' money ran out. The company's deed eventually passed to the British and then to the province.

TOP AND ABOVE
With closure of the Shubenacadie Canal in 1870, the parts of the water route nearest to Dartmouth became a popular summer destination for boating excursions and picnics.

OPPOSITE
The entrance to the Shubenacadie Canal at Dartmouth Cove circa 1892, just over twenty years after the canal was closed. The water level dropped significantly in this area after the closure of the canal.

The project was reactivated in 1853, with the incorporation of the Inland Navigation Company and the transfer of the assets of the Shubenacadie Canal Company. James Avery was named president, with William Stairs and George P. Mitchell as directors. The new company bought the property and works for £2,000, which was returned to them when the revived project was two-thirds complete. They petitioned the government for a further loan of £15,000 early in 1856, having paid for all work to date from their own funds. They also sought additional funds from their own shareholders in a preferred stock offering.[7]

The canal finally opened in 1857 with little fanfare and grudging press coverage.[8] The finished system consisted of seven locks and two ship railways, or inclined planes, one at Dartmouth and one between Lake Charles and Lake William. The first steamboat built to work the canal was the stern-wheeled paddle steamer *Avery*, built at Lower Lake Charles in 1856–57. At its peak there were three steamboats running in the canal.

Because they were owed significant sums of money for the canal's construction, John Stairs, George Starr, and Martin Black petitioned the Inland Navigation Company into bankruptcy. Shortly thereafter, they formed the Lake and River Navigation Company and took over the canal's assets in 1862. The canal operated until 1870, by which time the railway age had long since made it obsolete. To add insult to injury, a railway bridge was built across the Shubenacadie River in 1870, preventing any passage through the canal.[9]

SAMUEL CUNARD

The most famous Halifax shipowner of all, and perhaps the city's most famous son, was Samuel Cunard, who established the Cunard Line in 1839 to provide regular steamship service across

Shipping magnate Sir Samuel Cunard (1787–1865)

the Atlantic. Cunard was born in Halifax in 1787. In 1815, he started a mail service connecting Halifax, Newfoundland, Boston, and Bermuda. Prior to his investment in steamships, Cunard built a huge fleet of sailing vessels, owning at least seventy-six ships from 1817 to 1850. Like many other regional shipowners, he kept his vessels for a few years and sold them when he saw an opportunity for profit—a practice known as "buying cheap and selling dear."[10] As Phyllis Blakely writes, in the 1820s his vessels took part in the West Indies trade, "bringing in rum, molasses, sugar and some coffee, and carrying out dry and pickled fish, hoops and staves, mackerel, alewives, codfish, lumber, tea and oil."[11] They also imported dry goods, anchors, cables, and coal from Liverpool and London, and were active on the American East Coast, calling at Philadelphia for flour, meat, and fruit; at New York for corn, wheat, apples, nuts, and books; and at Boston for naval stores, flour, tobacco, and seeds.[12]

Cunard had a many-faceted career. The Miramichi timber trade with Britain, conducted as Joseph Cunard and Sons, was the foundation of his enterprise, but he was also involved in the Shubenacadie Canal, the Halifax Banking Company, and the Halifax Whaling Company. He was a shareholder in the Annapolis Iron Mining Company, and in 1825 he obtained the tea agency for the Maritime provinces from the East India Company, which allowed him to import tea and then re-export it to Newfoundland and the West Indies. The latter trade diminished in the 1830s due to increased competition from the Americans and a decline in sugar production, so Cunard expanded his business in Britain and bonded his Halifax warehouses for the use of other firms. In 1834, the General Mining Association, which owned the rights to all Nova Scotia coal, appointed Cunard as its local business agent and director of the corporation. In the late 1830s, he acquired two large estates on Prince Edward Island, and by the time of his

ABOVE
Cunard's Wharf as seen from the water, circa 1910

LEFT
The office and warehouse of S. Cunard & Company, which stood at 189–193 Upper Water Street until its demolition in November 1917

death in 1865, he was the single-largest landowner on the island.

Cunard was also attuned to new technologies that would transform shipping. As Phyllis Blakely points out, "as an alert shipowner, Cunard was aware of the development in steam vessels and noticed increasing numbers of such vessels at Liverpool and on the Irish Sea."[13] He and his brothers were amongst two hundred shareholders who took a financial interest in the Quebec and Halifax Steam Navigation Company, which built the early steamer *Royal William* in 1831 to serve the Halifax–Quebec route. Unfortunately, in 1833, the steamer was sold for less than one-third of its £16,000 delivery cost after being stuck in quarantine in Quebec.

By far, Cunard's most famous venture was his transatlantic steamship service, which car-

ABOVE
In 1833, ss *Royal William*, pictured here, became the first ocean steamer to cross the Atlantic, west to east, using only steam power.

OPPOSITE
RMS *Britannia*

ried passengers and the mail between Halifax and the U.K. The idea for the service came about in 1838, when the British Admiralty advertised for tenders to carry the mail by steam between Britain and New York via Halifax. Two tenders were received, but neither was satisfactory. Cunard only heard about the tender after the fact, at which point he sailed for England to plead his own case for an "ocean railroad." He offered to carry the mails from England to Halifax and back twice monthly using vessels of not less than 300 horsepower, and to provide two branch services, one to Boston and one between Pictou and Quebec, using smaller boats of 150 horsepower. He asked for a subsidy of £55,000 yearly for ten years, commencing May 1, 1840, and the Admiralty accepted his offer.

Cunard contacted shipbuilder Robert Napier for estimates of shipbuilding costs. Napier suggested he use larger vessels than he had originally planned and quoted a reduced price of £30,000, based on an order of three vessels. When Cunard experienced difficulty selling stock in his new enterprise, Napier introduced him to George Burns and the MacIver brothers, David and Charles, who became his partners, along with James Burns and Napier's brother Charles. Cunard was the lone Nova Scotian investor, putting up £67,500, while the two Burnses subscribed £5,000 each and the MacIver brothers invested £4,000 apiece. Thus,

the British and North American Royal Steam Packet Company was incorporated, and what became known as the Cunard Line was born. In Halifax, the populace was delighted to hear of Cunard's contract, and local businessmen raised £8,000 to build a hotel to accommodate the influx of passengers that would be visiting the city. On July 17, 1840, the first scheduled steamer, *Britannia*, stopped in Halifax with Cunard and his daughter on board, and quickly discharged its passengers before sailing on to Boston. The Bostonians had trumped Halifax by offering to build a pier and dock for easy transfer to rail in exchange for Cunard building larger vessels and calling at Boston with the same vessels that called at Halifax, rather than as a branch service.

After the successful launch of the steamship service in 1840, the Cunard family built or registered a further 64 sailing vessels of their grand total of 226 ships. These were built in New Brunswick, PEI, and across Halifax Harbour at the Lyle shipyard in Dartmouth.[14] Cunard's contract with the British Admiralty was renewed in 1846 for £145,000 per annum, by which time a competing bid had emerged from the Great Western Steamship Company of Bristol, headed by the brilliant Isambard Brunel.[15] The American Collins Line entered the fray in the 1850s, with larger, faster, and more luxurious vessels. In 1858, the government of the now-united Canadas attempted to have the contract for the St. Lawrence mail service transferred to the Allan Line, owned by Hugh Allan. Cunard prevailed, however, and a new contract was signed that year, calling for eight vessels of 400 horsepower, weekly service between Liverpool and New York, and fortnightly service to Halifax and Boston.

A bird's-eye view of Halifax Harbour, 1879

THE AGE OF SAIL

During the Age of Sail, the Halifax waterfront was a veritable forest of spars. It was dominated by as many as 180 wharves along the waterfront, stretching from Morris Street in the South End to Richmond Street in the North End. There were also several wharves dotting the Dartmouth shoreline. Other than military facilities, there was very little public investment in port infrastructure at this time, and the vast majority of wharves were privately owned.

However, despite the receipt of public investment funds, the military facilities in Halifax were beginning to decline. The British Naval Board moved the headquarters of the North Atlantic Station from Halifax to Bermuda in 1819, and the amount of stores retained in Halifax

HM Naval Yard, circa 1870

could only provision one ship, two frigates, and three sloops. The staff consisted only of a clerk, a boatswain, a gate porter, a painter, and six shipwrights. An additional twenty-six workers were added later in the year, but the facility was still greatly understaffed, as the skeleton staff was expected to look after a complex that consisted of thirty-three buildings. As historian Marilyn Gurney-Smith writes, from 1819 to 1907, "Halifax was no longer a major player in the defence of British North America against French and American attacks."[16] As maintenance money from Britain dried up, "the wharves were rotting, the storehouses and sail loft needed new roofs, and the wall was falling down," according to Gurney-Smith.[17] In 1832, the Naval Yard received a reprieve of sorts, when the Admiralty decided to establish a provision depot in Halifax and money for maintenance began to flow once again. During the 1850s, the regular fleet stationed at Halifax was between fifteen and seventeen ships.

THE "DARK SIDE"

There was also a "dark side" to life in nineteenth-century Halifax. In the words of Judith Fingard, "It had a working class underbelly found largely to the north, east and west of Citadel Hill, infested with grog shops, brothels, boarding houses and tenement accommodation for military dependents and the civilians who preyed upon the army."[18] A large number of taverns and sailors' boarding houses were located along Upper and Lower Water streets, causing the area to be dubbed "Sailortown." In Fingard's words, "it was the sailor's rowdiness which remained the best known feature of his port activities. He neatly fitted the stereotype of Jack ashore when he was involved in drunken brawls [and] when he was carried aboard his vessel senseless."[19] However, while Halifax possessed a large underclass, located mainly in the area around Barrack Street (now Brunswick Street), it was not a particularly violent city, and its citizens avoided the ethnic and political rioting that characterized other North American towns at this time.

Barrack Street (now Brunswick Street), 1884

The population of Canadian port cities swelled by hundreds, if not thousands, of men during the shipping season, as cargo handling was performed on a casual basis until the 1870s. Sailors themselves maintained a share of these duties until the 1890s, but there was

Seamen's Rest Home, 16–18 Upper Water Street, 1885

little fraternization between sailors and stevedores. There were few safety standards aboard vessels either at sea or in port, and loading and unloading cargoes was extremely dangerous, but attempts to unionize would not come until much later.

THE GATEWAY CONCEPT

In 1839, John George Lambton, Earl of Durham, first mentioned the idea of a railway linking the colonies of British North America in his famous *Report on the Affairs of British North America*. In 1845, a number of businessmen in London, backed by Samuel Cunard, proposed that such a railway be constructed. Unfortunately, as Phyllis Blakely explains, "The project collapsed amidst personal and political rivalries."[20] At this point, the government of Nova Scotia was merely wrestling with the idea of a railroad to link Halifax with Windsor and another one to link it with Truro. In the early 1850s, however, local politician and journalist Joseph Howe endorsed a scheme articulated by John A. Poor, a lawyer from Portland, Maine, who advocated the construction of a railway eastward to Bangor, Saint John, Halifax, and Canso.[21] The concept was very simple: join the two closest points in Europe (or Britain) to the closest port on mainland North America and offer regular and speedy steamship service. Howe argued in favour of a rail connection to Portland, Boston, and New York, "which would give to Nova Scotia and New Brunswick a noble highway through their territory, connect them by railway with all the principle cities on this continent and secure to the port selected for the eastern terminus, commercial advantages with which no seaport within the republic could ever successfully compete."[22] The full cost of the 330 miles (530 kilometres) of railway to Portland was estimated to be $12 million in 1850, and the 130 miles (210 kilometres) running through Nova Scotia would have been £800,000, or $4 million. Its construction would also give the British colonies the option to build a 670 mile (1,080 kilometre) "British" road connecting Halifax to Quebec City, with another 180 miles (290 kilometres) to Montreal, "rendering Halifax the great port of communication between the two continents of Europe and America," as Howe put it.[23] The colonial secretary, Earl Grey, flatly rejected Howe's entreaties for an imperial guarantee for the Quebec road and Howe turned his attention back towards the Portland scheme.

Howe pointed out that the Portland line would cost about half as much as the Quebec route and would connect Halifax and Saint John. Moreover, "the Portland railroad would secure to Nova Scotia the advantages which nature designed her to enjoy; connecting her with all the lines running through the American continent, and making Halifax a common terminus for them all."[24] Howe claimed that the route between Europe and America via a railroad connecting at Halifax would save every traveller fifty-six hours in travel time. In late 1850, Howe went to London to secure funds for the Portland railway, but returned five months later with a guarantee for an intercolonial railway wholly through British territory, instead. Upon his return to Nova Scotia, he found there was still support for the Portland option and, in New Brunswick, little for the Canadian route.[25] Howe argued that agreeing to build the Canadian route was the only hope for the Portland line and then somewhat unrealistically suggested that Nova Scotia, New Brunswick, and Quebec share equally in building the Quebec line, even though he knew that a scheme for a

Joseph Howe (1804–1873)

Windsor Station, part of the original Nova Scotia Railway, circa 1890

route along the east coast of New Brunswick would not receive the support of New Brunswick's commercial interests in Saint John. A delegation from the united Canadas and New Brunswick eventually came forward with a proposal for a line along the St. John River. They proposed that Nova Scotia pay for 159 miles (256 kilometres) in total, 29 miles (47 kilometres) more than passed through the province. Howe got approval from the legislature to borrow £800,000 and to arrange for the construction of one-quarter of the total length of the line.

Parts of Howe's scheme were built in fits and starts over a twenty-five-year period, but Howe and Poor's grand vision of a single line linking Halifax with Portland, Boston, and New York was never fully realized. In the 1850s, two railways were built in Nova Scotia, one to Windsor and the other to Truro. In New Brunswick, the St. Andrews and Quebec Railway (SA&Q) was built between St. Andrews and Debec in 1856, and the European and North American Railway (E&NA) was completed between Saint John and Pointe de Chêne, near Shediac, in 1860. In 1869, it was incorporated into the Intercolonial Railway, which would link Halifax with Quebec by 1876. The early railroads of the 1850s expanded Halifax's hinterland, but only marginally. It was a major weakness that took years of effort to overcome.

THE "GOLDEN AGE" AND U.S. CIVIL WAR

Nova Scotia was a relatively prosperous and sophisticated place in the mid-nineteenth century, and it had the region's most diversified economy, including shipbuilding, shipping, fishing, and coal mining. But in spite of the province's fairly strong economy, Halifax still paled in comparison to Saint John, its rival across the Bay of Fundy. Saint John was the largest city in the region and only eclipsed by Montreal and Quebec City in British North America. It was the biggest shipbuilding centre in the Maritimes and one of the leading shipowning ports in the world. Lacking a natural hinterland comparable to the Saint John River valley, Halifax was no match for Saint John economically.

However, the Reciprocity Treaty of 1854, inaugurating free trade in "natural products" with the U.S., resulted in a trade boom that had a major impact on Halifax's economy. The colony's exports almost tripled from 1850 to 1857, most likely due to the advent of reciprocity. Although opinions differ as to whether this period really was a "golden age," there is little doubt that Nova Scotia had the region's most diversified economy.

The U.S. Civil War, from 1861 to 1865, brought further benefits to Halifax's economy, mostly rising from Britain's position of official "neutrality" in the war. Maritime merchants, and those in Halifax in particular, while not necessarily supporters of the South, were not shy about taking advantage of commercial opportunities afforded by the conflict. As Greg Marquis explains, "The Civil War was more a blessing than a curse. Nova Scotia exports to the U.S. doubled in value between 1861 and 1865."[26] Although they were unable to trade with the Southern states, Nova Scotian exporters of lumber, fish, and minerals did do a fair amount of business with the Northern states, which were undergoing a period of rapid industrialization during the Civil War era. Shipbuilding and shipowning were very profitable during this time, and in the first year of the war, the three Maritime colonies launched a total of 260 vessels. In the last year of the war, 560 vessels came out of Maritime shipyards.

The Union blockade declared in April 1861, which closed nearly 3,600 miles (5,800 kilometres) of rebel coastline to British shipping, was one of the major causes of support for the Confederacy in British North America. Many interests considered the blockade a violation of the Reciprocity Treaty, as it effectively closed the Southern U.S. market to exports of fish, lumber, plaster (gypsum), and potatoes. Maritime shipowners and the Port of Halifax did benefit, however, from West Indies sugar and molasses transshipped through Halifax and then distributed to U.S. markets in the North. Likewise, Halifax was often used as a staging point for blockade-runners supplying the Confederates with munitions, arms, medicine, and other cargo.[27]

BENJAMIN WIER

One notable participant in Confederate trade was Benjamin Wier, a Halifax merchant, politician, shipowner, and Confederate sympathizer who owned a wharf and warehouse located between Sackville and Salter streets. His firm, Wier and Co., specialized in trading with New

England, exporting fish and importing American foodstuffs, tobacco, tar, and other staples. In 1847, Wier started a packet run between Halifax and Boston, with two small sailing vessels making regular trips. In the 1850s, he expanded his enterprise to include a fleet of vessels that traded at ports all over the Gulf of St. Lawrence, bringing supplies from Halifax to the outports and returning with fish, oil, and timber, which were later exported to New England.

When the Civil War broke out, Wier found a profitable enterprise in the Confederate supply effort, acting as an agent for the Confederate authorities. Wier provided Confederate blockade-runners with the use of his ship repair facilities, and in return they provided him with Southern cotton, which he shipped out to Britain for a considerable profit. However, this new business venture meant that he had to break off his relationships with firms in New England, and when the Confederacy collapsed at the end of the Civil War, he found himself *persona non grata* with the American authorities and unable to travel to the U.S. However, despite his ostracism from the U.S., Wier eventually managed to secure the agency for a steamer service connecting Halifax with the Grand Trunk terminal in Portland, Maine.[28]

TALLAHASSEE

Wier was also involved in perhaps the most famous Civil War incident in Halifax: the dramatic escape of the blockade-runner *Tallahassee* through Eastern Passage. *Tallahassee* was a fast twin-screw steamship and one of the most feared Southern raiders.[29] In the summer of 1864, it burned or bonded over thirty vessels on its initial cruise. After pillaging commercial vessels, immigrant ships, pilot boats, and fishing schooners off the eastern seaboard for more than ten days, the vessel's skipper, John Taylor Wood, headed for the neutral port of Halifax to refuel.

TOP
The Confederate steamship *Tallahassee*

ABOVE
Vice Admiral Sir James Hope

Upon entering Halifax Harbour, the skipper anchored his vessel off Market Wharf. Haligonians, even though they were by now quite accustomed to seeing Confederate warships, gathered on the many wharves and jetties in the vicinity to catch a glimpse.

Tallahassee's skipper respected protocol and visited the senior Royal Navy officer in Halifax, Vice Admiral Sir James Hope. Wood had a brief interview with Hope and was told that he had twenty-four hours to re-coal and that he could not purchase munitions while in port. The u.s. consul, Mortimer Jackson, attempted to persuade the Nova Scotia authorities to detain *Tallahassee* or prevent it from taking on coal, hoping to prove it had violated international law. The lieutenant-governor, suspecting that Jackson merely wanted to delay the vessel's departure until Union gunboats arrived, replied that he had no jurisdiction in the matter. However, he limited *Tallahassee*'s coal intake to just enough fuel to get the ship to its nearest home port, Wilmington, North Carolina.

While preparing to leave Halifax, Wood declined the offer of a naval escort to the three-mile limit, sensing he'd be met by Union gunboats. As Greg Marquis writes, "He was thinking more like a blockade runner than warship commander," and instead he decided to depart under the cover of darkness through the seldom used and potentially hazardous Eastern Passage.[30] Thanks to Jock Flemming, a harbour pilot from Halifax, who assured Wood that he could guide the ship through the passage "with the bottom only touching eel grass," *Tallahassee* glided past the inner harbour, passing Queen's Wharf and the ordnance yard, the gun batteries at Point Pleasant, and McNab's and Lawlor's islands before clearing the easternmost harbour approaches at Devil's Island.[31] Contrary to local lore, Union vessels did not arrive until after *Tallahassee* made good its escape. Because of the limited amount of bunkers he was able to load, Wood sailed directly to Wilmington, but rumours persisted for weeks that Halifax Harbour and the coast of Nova Scotia were thick with Union gunboats searching for *Tallahassee*.

CONFEDERATION

In the early- to mid-1860s, the idea of uniting the Province of Canada (itself a union of the former Upper Canada and Lower Canada) with the Maritime colonies, known as Confederation, began to gain appeal. In the run-up to Confederation, "Canadian" politicians who were proponents of the union, including Georges Etienne Cartier and John A. Macdonald, made numerous promises relating to the Port of Halifax in order to gain Nova Scotia's support. In September 1864, Cartier promised that "Halifax, through the Intercolonial Railroad, [would] be the recipient of trade which [then] benefit[ed] Portland, Boston and New York."[32] He went on to predict that a daily steamer, "like a ferry," would soon connect Halifax and Liverpool. With the usual hyperbole of the time, but which Haligonians took literally, Macdonald proclaimed, "Build the road and Halifax will soon become one of the great

Jock Flemming

ABOVE
Sir John A. Macdonald

OPPOSITE
The Union Bank of Halifax

emporiums of the world. All the great resources of the West will come over the immense railways of Canada to the bosom of your harbour."[33] A. T. Galt, the minister of finance for the Canadas, echoed these sentiments, promising that Canada would no longer enrich American ports, but would build up the ports of Halifax and Saint John instead. George Brown, politician and proprietor of Toronto's *Globe* newspaper, said the Intercolonial Railway would "make Halifax and Saint John the Atlantic seaports of half a continent."[34] Brown also predicted a steady stream of passengers and immigrants passing through the "lower provinces." Even though there had been comparatively little trade between the Canadas and the Maritime provinces prior to 1867, the idea of building a railway connecting the colonies of British North America had been discussed since 1839, and the notion of Halifax becoming the gateway to the British-controlled portion of the continent would have had considerable appeal. But the politicians' promises would prove to be empty; Confederation would not bring the changes Haligonians had been promised.

At the time of Confederation in 1867, Halifax was a city of close to 29,000 people in a province of about 390,000. Halifax was the fourth-largest city in the new dominion, after Montreal, Quebec City, and Toronto, having surpassed its long-time rival Saint John in the previous decade. From a commercial viewpoint, the main business of the city was still shipping and trade. Reflecting this, Halifax was home to five indigenous banks, including the Halifax Banking Company, the Bank of Nova Scotia, the Union Bank of Halifax, the Merchants' Bank of Halifax, and the People's Bank of Halifax.

Phyllis Blakely eloquently described the mood in Halifax at the time of Confederation:

Looking at its magnificent harbour, and its wharves crowded with shipping, few dared to believe that the golden age of wood, wind and sail was drawing to a close. The wharves along Halifax harbour were piled high with sugar, molasses, rum and fruit from the West Indies; manufactured articles of all kinds from England; fish, lumber, coal and agricultural produce from Cape Breton, Prince Edward Island and New Brunswick.[35]

Ironically, the Cunard Line, whose founder had died two years before, ceased calling at Halifax the same month as Confederation because of insufficient traffic levels. It was not a good omen.

CHAPTER THREE

The Wharf of the Dominion
1867–1913

No other economic issues better exemplified Halifax's aspirations, and its frustrations, with Confederation than the so-called "winter port" and "fast line" debates. Proponents of the winter port concept stressed the benefit of having mail and cargo destined for Canadian markets delivered through Canadian ports during the winter. The proposed service would consist of a line of steamers running direct routes between Halifax and the U.K., without stopping at American ports. They argued that mail, cargo, and passengers could be transported to and from the other Canadian provinces and the northeastern United States via the ICR, thus eliminating the need to have Canadian goods shipped through American ports. The lobbying for winter port status reached its first crescendo around 1880. Halifax's boosters waged a tireless campaign, only to be confronted with the harsh new reality of Confederation. At first, they demanded that any contracts given for the carriage of Canadian mails to and from the U.K. must also require the carriage of passengers and freight from Halifax

ABOVE
Sir Hugh Allan

OPPOSITE
The railway line along Bedford Basin, which connected Halifax with markets in western Canada

to Liverpool at a rate one-sixth less than the prevailing rates from U.S. ports, since Halifax was closer to the U.K. than the nearest U.S. port by that distance.[1] Then, in 1879, Halifax shipping agent George P. Black proposed that the Montreal-based Allan Line stop calling at Baltimore and turn its vessels at Halifax, thus saving $100,000 annually by sailing a shorter distance. He may have been the first to articulate a long-held dream of Halifax: "this difference in our favour…could… convince the shippers of Chicago and other places in the West…that by shipping on through bills of lading via Halifax they would get their grain to Liverpool at 1¾d. sterling per quarter less than by any other route."[2]

The key to the argument was not only the shorter distance between Halifax and Liverpool, but also port costs, which were much less in Halifax than in comparable American ports. In March 1880, Sir Hugh Allan offered to spend up to $250,000 of his own money to build a large wharf complex in Dartmouth and run the Allan Line between Liverpool and Halifax. His offer was contingent upon the federal government extending the Intercolonial Railway into Dartmouth and giving him a long-term contract to carry the mail. Not only would this have benefited local industry, it also would have alleviated the ICR's losses, estimated at $500,000 per annum, by increasing the volume of freight, passengers, and mail running across it.[3]

Allan's offer was never accepted, even though it appeared to address most of Halifax's concerns. It was estimated that the extension of the ICR into Dartmouth would cost $270,000, and would have resulted in having railway operations on both sides of the harbour, and thus meant additional expense.[4] Despite this disappointing setback and apparently lost opportunity, Halifax's port boosters kept up the pressure. In words that have a familiar ring today, they sang Halifax's praises: "The Port of Halifax is without peer, and is unexceptionably the finest and

ABOVE
Halifax Harbour from the Citadel featuring George's Island, centre, and Dartmouth shore, top left, circa 1880s

OPPOSITE
Looking north up Halifax Harbour toward Bedford Basin from the spire of St. Mary's Cathedral, circa 1880s

most commodious in the world, is easy of access, and free from all dangers and obstruction to shipping, and the closest point to Europe on the American continent, and from its geographical position on the Atlantic seaboard, it is the wharf, as it were, of British America."[5]

Despite much effort on the part of Halifax port boosters, and some movement on freight rates on the part of the ICR, in late October 1880 the Allan Line announced that it would carry the Canadian mails via Boston, and that Canadian cargo via Halifax would be subject to the same rate as that via Boston. The company's ships would call at Halifax both inbound from the U.K. and outbound to the U.K., but it was hardly what had been expected.

In response to Halifax interests, the minister of railways had effected a number of changes with a view towards encouraging the movement of additional traffic along the ICR, including the enlargement of wharves and sheds and the reduction of freight rates on grain, so as to encourage return cargoes for the Allan Line and others. Even the secretary of railways and canals clashed with the Allans over their decision, yet it does not seem that it ever occurred to him or the government to require Canadian mails to travel via Canadian ports, especially when they benefited from government subsidy.[6] It was a much different situation from that in the U.S., where American shipping, ports, and shipbuilding were actively promoted. The decision upset members of the Halifax Chamber of Commerce, one of whom argued:

ABOVE
Postcard showing Piers 7 and 8. Note how the caption describes Halifax as the "Winter Port of Canada."

OPPOSITE
The Halifax waterfront, showing Robins Wharf at 105 Lower Water Street

In future, when taking tenders for the carrying of the mails, might it not be worthy [of] the consideration of the government, the advisability of stipulating that any line tendering must be prepared to make Halifax its terminal point during the winter months.

Were such a policy pursued and the interests of the Intercolonial Railway identified with the ocean line of steamers, I cannot but think it would result in a fairly remunerative trade to both, while, at the same time, it would bring about the promise so temptingly held out at the time of Confederation, and during the building of the Intercolonial Railway, not to mention those so freely made during the last election campaign, of making Halifax the winter port of the Dominion.[7]

The impact of Allan's decision was predictable. Very little freight was either loaded or discharged at Halifax during his vessels' brief calls at the port. Most Canadian cargo and passengers were transported via Boston, since the rate was the same and the overland rail distance was shorter. As Halifax member of Parliament M. B. Daly wrote to Charles Tupper, minister of railways and canals, it was soon apparent that the Allans intended to give "all the freight they [could] to the Vermont Central [Railway] rather than the Intercolonial Railway."[8]

Allan's self-serving reply ignored the case that the Halifax proponents have long argued,

OPPOSITE
An assortment of vintage vessels—steamer, tall ship, and luxury liner—as seen from Pier 2, Halifax

namely that the city's closer proximity to Europe should be an advantage reflected in the rates charged on ocean freight and passengers, so as to compensate for the longer distance travelled by rail. Instead, Allan pointed to the small market for both freight and passenger traffic in Halifax, and ignored the potential advantage of landing both at Halifax and dispatching them on their way inland before the vessels had even docked in Boston. Undoubtedly, he wanted the additional revenue from the longer ocean haul to Boston, which he would have had to sacrifice if he lowered the rates to Halifax.

In an attempt to get Allan to reconsider his plans, many shippers provided evidence that their freight was expedited to Montreal much more quickly via Halifax than Boston, where even perishables would often languish on the docks for weeks before being transferred to their ultimate destination, while freight would arrive via Halifax and the ICR within three days.[9] Moreover, Allan's Canadian-bound freight was discharged in Boston at a pier that was not accessible to the rail head, necessitating a costly and time-consuming haul across the city. But this was not enough to sway Allan. And, to add insult to injury, subsequent investigations later revealed that his agents were actually charging more to land passengers in Halifax than in Boston.[10]

A NEW REALITY

Around the same time that Haligonian businessmen and politicians were lobbying for direct winter service between Halifax and the U.K., a committee of six members of the Halifax Chamber of Commerce also argued for the establishment of grain-handling facilities at Halifax, pointing out that "the enormous sum disbursed annually in the United States by our vessels would to a large extent be retained within the country...and would keep the

A south-facing view of the Halifax Harbour approaches as seen from the spire of St. Mary's Cathedral, with a portion of McNab's Island visible to the left and York Redoubt to the right in the far distance

produce of our great West from seeking an outlet to European markets over American roads, and through American ports."[11] They also argued that the government, which owned and ran the Intercolonial, should build special railcars to carry Nova Scotian coal westbound and western grain eastbound, thus making both cargoes more competitive in their respective markets and improving the ICR's financial position. They urged Sir John A. Macdonald's government to build a grain elevator in Halifax so that shipments could commence, as their canvassing of local shipowners led them to believe that vessels could be found to transport the grain[12] and a significant trade would arise if an elevator were to be built. This, in turn, would have a positive impact on the region's shipowners.[13]

Even though all six committee members were wealthy gentlemen, the Toronto-based *Monetary Times* noted that investing their own money in the scheme never seemed to occur to them. In their defence, it should be pointed out that it was customary at the time for railways to invest in their own terminal infrastructure, and that it would have been very rare for a private elevator to have been constructed without participation from either a grain or elevator company.[14] Given the amounts already expended on railway and canal construction in the Canadas, it was perhaps reasonable for Halifax to expect the government's assistance, which it considered to be its reward for joining Confederation. The government's reply, as written by David Pottinger, general manager of the ICR, was, however, a classic conundrum: "I cannot recommend the erection of elevators until it has been established that a grain traffic can be successfully conducted over the Intercolonial Railway with the Port of Halifax."[15] To his credit, Collingwood Schreiber, the government's chief railway engineer, did say that "in the absence of an elevator, a large steamer would scarcely undertake to put a cargo of grain as it would necessarily be attended with considerable delay."[16] However, he dashed the hopes of Halifax when he stated:

> I foresaw that it would lead to trouble if more favourable arrangements were made with one steamship company than with another, and the owning of elevators by a steamship company which was working under a specially favourable division of rates with the railways, would virtually give that company a monopoly, and be a ground for complaint.[17]

Despite the initial difficulties in procuring funding for the project, a grain elevator was eventually built at the foot of Cornwallis Street in 1882. It was destroyed by fire in 1895 and a replacement, with capacity for 600,000 bushels, was built three years later.

MOUNTING FRUSTRATION

In 1880, after passing a resolution citing the pre-Confederation promise to make Halifax the winter port of the Dominion, Halifax City Council requested that future federal subsidies for the carriage of mail require that mail be discharged at a Canadian port. Shortly thereafter, council also took matters into its own hands by waiving all port and customs charges for ships loading grain at Halifax, in expectation of, and as encouragement for, a decision to build a grain eleva-

ABOVE
Shipping wharves and rail lines at Richmond, circa 1890

OPPOSITE
Railcars line the tracks in this late nineteenth-century image looking north along Upper Water Street.

tor.[18] These civic initiatives emphasized the overall national benefit of having a thriving Atlantic gateway. In the meantime, the ICR began to promote the Halifax gateway with shippers in both the United Kingdom and Ontario. They also worked on fine-tuning their Halifax operation so that it resembled a modern-day "just-in-time" operation. As David Pottinger described:

> The mail steamer arrives at Halifax, discharges the mails at Cunard's wharf, and then goes down to our wharf at Richmond where she commences discharging her Canadian cargo. All the time the cargo is being discharged, it is being loaded into cars and sent off, so that when the steamer has discharged the last of her freight and leaves the wharf, all that is remaining in the stores to be despatched is the few car-loads just landed before she left the wharf. What she landed first would be a long distance on its way to Chaudière, and the whole of the freight that she landed will have arrived…before the steamer can possibly, under the most favourable circumstances, reach Boston.[19]

Once the ICR began to aggressively promote the Halifax routing, freight volumes grew over the winter, reaching 603 tons by mid-January 1881. Nonetheless, the Allan Line continued to downplay the all-Canadian route. The company's winter advertisements failed even to mention a Halifax port call, much to the ICR's chagrin.[20] Allan's people pleaded ignorance of the situation, choosing to blame their U.K. agents for the oversight. A few days later, Allan announced that henceforth his company's Glasgow steamers would call at Halifax en route to Boston, and attributed the increase in business via Halifax solely to his own, and not the railway's efforts.[21]

Haligonians considered winter port status, and the investment this would require in

56   CANADA'S ATLANTIC GATEWAY

THE WHARF OF THE DOMINION, 1867-1913

grain-handling facilities, to be their birthright. In the words of "Haligonian," an anonymous correspondent to the *Monetary Times*,

> When $50,000,000 are being spent for a railway in the North West, and $20,000,000 are being expended on the canals in widening and improving them, in which we have no interest, is it asking too much of the government to spend…as much even as the Erie and Tunnel railways are expending on their terminus at Boston, to fully equip the Intercolonial railway terminus at Halifax?[22]

The *Monetary Times* argued that the ICR should pay its own way without subsidy, while Halifax business people argued that the ICR should be given every chance to succeed, including mandating the carriage of Canadian mails over its length. To them, it made as much sense to send Canadian cargo via Boston as it would to send it to the Pacific Northwest via Duluth and Chicago. Barely thirteen years after Confederation, "Haligonian" bitterly commented: "Confederation has hitherto been too one-sided, and we, down here, are desirous of seeing a change and would not even regret a return to a separate existence."[23]

The *Monetary Times* was not impressed. Its editors accused Halifax of having "not moved a finger to secure this great prize."[24] Ignoring all the port's advantages, the editors concluded that geography was not on its side and that it was too far from inland markets compared with its competitors. However, the paper did concede that the ICR had been built "rather for political, imperial and military than for commercial purposes, and that no one need be surprised if the difficulty of making it a commercial success is very great."[25] It was a statement that would prove to be very prophetic.

THE FAST LINE

A few months after the federal election of 1891, in which native Haligonian John S. D. Thompson was elected as prime minister, Halifax MP John F. Stairs returned to the winter port and related fast line issue. A prominent financier and industrialist, Stairs lobbied Sir John Abbott, president of the Privy Council and future prime minister, on behalf of his constituents. Throughout the fall, he wrote Abbott and Prime Minister Thompson numerous memos on the fast line and winter port issues, which he considered interlinked. His basic argument was that allowing a subsidized mail steamer to call at an American port "really means that you pay them to take freight to and from that port."[26] Moreover, the existing contract with the Allan Line resulted in freight from the Maritime provinces being shut out, much to the detriment of local shippers, since by the time the company's vessels arrived from Portland, they were fully loaded. The inbound voyage was not a problem, except that little freight for the "Upper Provinces" had been landed at Halifax for many years, most of it having been shipped via Portland. As Stairs envisioned it, the fast line of steamers to run between the U.K. and Halifax would carry mail, passengers, and a limited amount of high-value freight:

> It must not be forgotten that a large trade with England is being developed in articles that require rapid transit and that can pay for rates, this naturally would go by the fast line. On staple articles the steamers might have to take a proportionately lower rate from Halifax than from New York, but in compensation about a day and a quarter would be saved in her voyage.[27]

Although an experienced and oftentimes brilliant businessman, Stairs also advanced the naïve notion that "distance does not form as much of an element in the rates as those unacquainted with railway management would imagine."[28] He contended that the availability of substantial amounts of long-haul traffic was equally important and that requiring the mail contractor to land passengers, mail, and freight at Halifax would achieve this end. As an alternative to the Allan Line, which seemed more and more committed to Portland, he suggested that the government sound out the now Liverpool-based Cunard Line, as their vessels were better and faster.[29]

Mindful of the potential political fallout, Abbott consulted numerous experts and other politicians prior to making any decision. Unfortunately, at least one of them, and perhaps the most important one, was entirely unsympathetic to Halifax's cause; CPR president Sir William Van Horne's rebuttal of Stairs's proposal was very disappointing. Although the CPR had completed its so-called Short Line to Saint John in 1889, the concept of using a Canadian port on the East Coast seemed completely lost on its president. The CPR had, in the past decade, received at least $25 million and 25 million acres of what would become prime real estate to build a Canadian outlet to the Pacific. His response completely dismissed a whole city's (and, by implication, a whole region's) aspirations:

> I am quite unable to see what practical advantage it can be to Halifax to have the freight of the upper Provinces handled [there]; it means the employment of a few more wharf labourers and nothing more that I can see. The question must largely be a sentimental one. If the ships go to Halifax in the winter and discharge their passengers, mails and express freight, and are there ready again to make their departure at the time fixed by the contract, I cannot see what difference it can make to the country or to Halifax.[30]

At a subsequent meeting with Van Horne at the Windsor Hotel in Montreal, Stairs presented his case for the fast line. Stairs recommended that the line call at Liverpool in the U.K., Halifax during the winter, and either Quebec City or Montreal during the summer. To the suggestion that a substantial additional subsidy would be required to turn the vessels at Halifax, he countered that the owners would require less fuel and incur lower port charges by making the switch, which would be reflected in their overall operating costs. He estimated the additional cost "for the sake of securing an absolutely Canadian line" to be in the vicinity of $110,000 per annum.[31] Of critical importance to Stairs's argument was the speed of the vessels, which would allow them to compete for passenger traffic with services out of New York and take full advantage of Halifax's geographical location and shorter steaming time.

Stairs acknowledged that there were some difficulties in terms of gaining access to markets in the U.S. Midwest, but he reminded Abbott that "every argument which was advanced against the fast line was of the same nature as those which were advanced against the construction of the Canadian Pacific," and appealed to him to establish a Canadian line to prevent Canada from drifting into commercial union with the U.S.[32] Once the fast line was established, Stairs predicted that Canada would no more want to be without its own fast line of steamers than without a railway to the Pacific. He was sorely mistaken.

MORE DISAPPOINTMENT

Within days of his meeting with Abbott, Stairs learned of his own government's intention once again to award the winter mail contract to the Allan Line via Portland, thus bypassing Halifax altogether and eliminating all mail service to the city.[33] His arguments had fallen on deaf ears. Writing to Prime Minister Thompson, Stairs called for the subsidy to the Allans to be withdrawn and the mails to be sent via New York, where better and cheaper service was available without the need for subsidy.[34] A desperate Stairs urged Thompson to make a temporary arrangement with Cunard, Dominion, or, as a last resort, Allan, to provide some service to Halifax during the winter.

In the ensuing weeks, Stairs continued to hammer away at his main points, that "the government's policy must be to build up Canadian ports, and to discourage in every possible way, those of the United States" and that the best ways to do so were through the mail subsidy and the development of a fast line of steamers. Stairs was joined in his efforts by the Halifax Board of Trade and the Labourer's Union of Halifax. The issue also caused some concern in Saint John, especially with George Foster, the minister of finance and one of the local MPs from that city. More negotiations ensued, and new tenders were issued for winter mail service to Halifax and Saint John, with a further complication: the addition of a French port. It was agreed to develop tenders for a fast line, but these once again got bogged down in details such as port selection and vessel speed. To Stairs's chagrin, the question of calling at a U.S. port remained unresolved. Clearly frustrated, he poured out his and his constituents' feelings to Abbott:

> I do not see how any Canadian who believes in Canadian unity and independence of the United States commercially or politically could support a vote that means the building up of American ports and railways in preference to Canadian.
>
> Portland was largely built up by the subsidy paid by the Canadian people and you can never secure the Canadian trade for Canadian ports as long as you permit subsidies to be paid to steamers to a United States port.[35]

In the interim, on behalf of S. M. Brookfield, a Halifax building contractor, Stairs called for a subsidy for the Halifax, Liverpool & London Steamship Company, which proposed to operate between Liverpool, Halifax, and Saint John using the vessels *Ulunda* and *Barcelona*. The company aimed to serve exporters in the Maritimes who were not well served during the summer months, and only marginally served by the Allan and Dominion lines in winter.[36] He suggested that the subsidy expire upon the establishment of the fast line, so that these kinds of expenditures would not be too financially onerous. To justify the subsidy, he cited the numerous spinoffs that would benefit the Canadian economy, including stevedoring, provisioning, crew wages, and additional traffic for the ICR. In 1893, the Halifax, Liverpool & London Steamship Company received a grant from the Newfoundland government to carry the mail between Halifax, St. John's, and Liverpool on a year-round basis, at which time the company was transformed into the Canada and Newfoundland Steamship Company.

SIGNS OF HOPE

Work on the ICR's Deep Water Terminal had commenced in 1877, just after the railway itself became operational. Its construction "in an area of high quality housing drove affluent households to seek refuge on the western side of the peninsula," according to historian Jay White.[37] It would not be the last time port development would have such an impact. The terminal was completed in 1882 after an expenditure of $174,000. By 1900, twelve ocean steamers could dock at Deep Water, and as White notes,

This 1894 map of Halifax provides a graphic frame of reference for the Intercolonial Railway Station, H. M. Dockyard, Deep Water Terminal, and the Engineers Yard and R. N. S. Yacht Squadron, where the Ocean Terminals were built in the early 1900s.

ABOVE
Deep Water Terminal and the replacement grain elevator built in the North End of Halifax

OPPOSITE
Deep Water Terminal, showing Pier 3, centre, with portions of Piers 2 and 4 visible to the sides, circa 1905

"the piers and docks were repaired and enlarged until the wharves stretched along Upper Water Street south of the Dockyard between Gerrish and Cornwallis Streets."[38] A total of $500,000 had been expended in the process.

After years of frustration, the amount of cargo handled at the port doubled in the 1890s, and passenger traffic grew substantially. In the last six months of 1898, by Phyllis Blakely's count, about 1,600 carloads of "deals, pulp, shooks, eggs, butter, flour, bacon, cheese, grain, leather and canned goods were shipped to Britain," while 470 cars of "flour, corn, pork, hay, fish, potatoes and shingles were shipped to the West Indies."[39] That same year, the port handled 934 inbound vessels and 1,005 outbound ships, carrying a total of 1.2 million tons of cargo. By the turn of the century, Halifax had an impressive roster of shipping lines serving a multitude of markets. Furness-Withy, Dominion, Allan, Manchester, Beaver, and the Hamburg-American lines served the European trade. The Pickford and Black fleet "ran to Bermuda, Havana and Jamaica carrying fish, potatoes, flour and farm produce to the West Indies, and bringing in return pimento, ginger, coffee, bitterwood, logwood and rum," according to Blakely.[40] The Red Cross Line ran from New York to Newfoundland, and the Plant Line operated from Halifax to Boston during the summer.

A NEW ERA

The turn of the century brought further developments at the Port of Halifax. As it had done for many years, the Board of Trade continued to lobby relentlessly for improved harbour facilities, freight rate parity with competing Atlantic ports, and the use of steamer subsidies to attract traffic.[41] The board also had a joint committee with the City of Halifax, which dealt with the issue of port development and promotion. In 1911, the committee recommended that the harbour be placed under commission control, like the harbours of Quebec, Montreal, and Toronto. It also recommended the purchase of land to the south of Deep Water Terminal and the construction of three large piers. Despite Halifax's apparent success at attracting immigrant vessels, these new facilities were needed because, as Thomas Raddall put it, the "huge new liners on the North Atlantic could not be berthed at all."[42]

When Halifax lawyer Robert L. Borden became prime minister in 1911, the port finally received the kind of attention to which it had long aspired, and which Borden had previously outlined in a 1903 speech on government railway policy.[43] Except for a letter to Wilfrid Laurier in 1911, Borden's papers contain no hint of the motivation behind what was to come, nor of the scale he envisioned.[44] However, having been immersed in the Halifax legal community prior to becoming MP and prime minister, he would have been familiar with Halifax's frustration and ambition to become a North Atlantic entrepôt. Borden had agreed wholeheartedly with the Board of Trade's plan for the harbour, and while he was the MP for Halifax, he had urged Laurier to act on it. At the time, the port could only accommodate twelve to sixteen steamships at once, which was not considered adequate. In June 1913, Borden came to Halifax to meet with representatives of the Board of Trade, who urged him to proceed with the plans they had envisioned.

ABOVE
The Pickford and Black Wharf on the Halifax waterfront

OPPOSITE
The Plant Steamship Company wharf and building at the foot of Sackville Street, Halifax. The Plant Line, established in Halifax in 1889, dominated the cargo and passenger run between Halifax and Boston because it provided the only direct, non-stop service.

Prime Minister Robert Borden, fourth from left, inspects the new Ocean Terminal project in 1916

Four months later, in October 1913, the long-awaited announcement that the federal government would study the potential for new investment in the Port of Halifax was made by Frank Cochrane, the minister of railways.

The port also had a good year in terms of traffic, and attracted three new lines, including Cunard, which came back into the fold after an absence of forty-six years. As well, after many years of trying to entice them, the Allan Line had finally decided to make Halifax its winter port, "the advent of service predicted long ago, but now realized," as the Board of Trade put it.[45]

THE COWIE REPORT

Between 1912 and 1913, Frederick Cowie, a consulting engineer from Montreal, studied several proposals to massively increase federal government investment in cargo-handling facilities in Halifax. Cowie had been to Halifax in 1904, when he had accompanied the minister of marine and fisheries on an inspection tour intended to provide ideas for improving port facilities. At that point, most of the waterfront was still privately owned, and Cowie immediately identified a major problem with the existing publicly constructed facilities, which were located at Richmond in the North End and at Deep Water Terminal at the foot of Cornwallis Street; they offered poor access to the city, no connecting sites for warehouses or industry, and no marshalling areas for railway and steamship traffic.

Cowie thought Halifax had many advantages. It was the best terminal port in North America for fast transatlantic mail and passenger services and the closest port to Europe. It was a safe and easily accessible winter port for Canada and it was a year-round port of call for shipping between Europe and North America. The inner harbour was only a 19.5-nautical-mile deviation off the Great Circle Route from Europe to New York. He was amongst the first (though not the last) to declare that "passengers discharged at Halifax en route to Chicago arrived in Chicago just as the passengers who stayed on the vessel would board the train in New York." The only complaint of captains of vessels calling at Halifax was the state of the port's facilities. Cowie thought that with improved facilities, Halifax would enjoy a huge increase in use as a terminal port and a port of call. He advocated the development of terminal facilities and warehouses suitable for the products and natural resources of the province, "so that a reliable and steady market may be assured for the products of the fisheries, market gardens, orchards and pastures."[46]

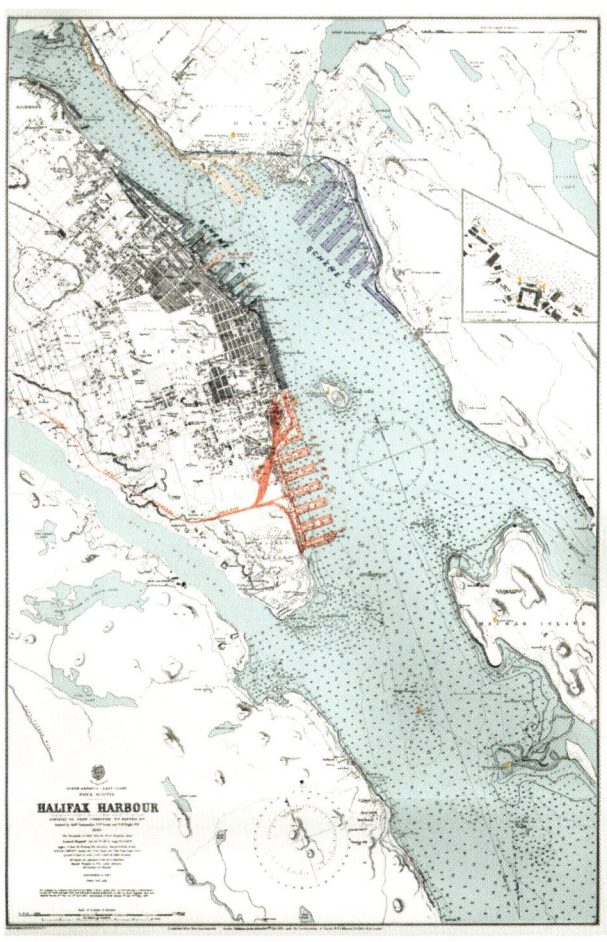

A 1913 map from the Cowie Report showing the proposed Ocean Terminals development

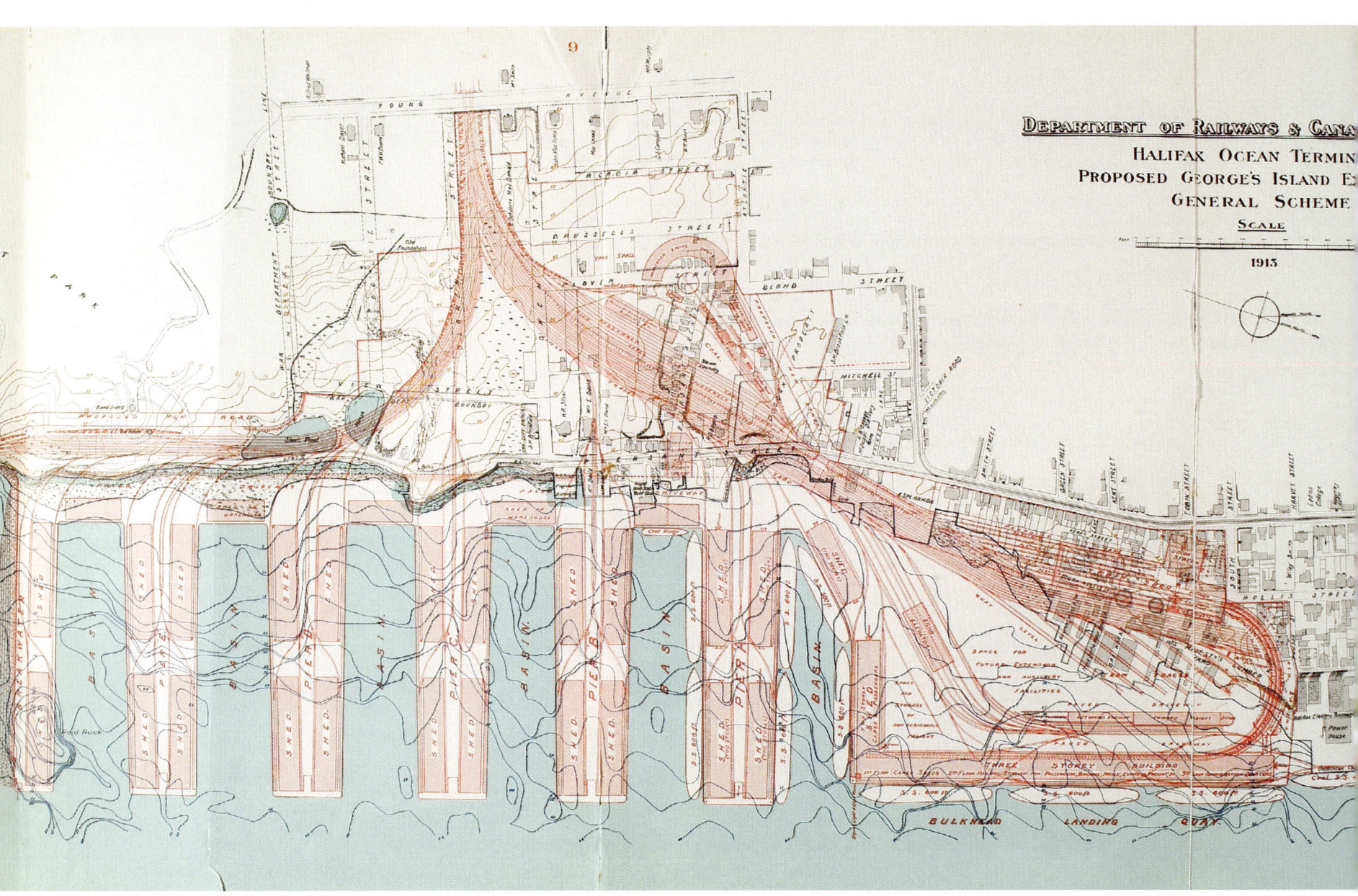

The Cowie Report of 1913 discussed four alternative sites for the development of what would eventually be called the Ocean Terminals. These included the foot of Cunard Street (at the Deep Water Terminal site), Tufts Cove, Dartmouth Cove, and a site called George's Island, which was located in the area opposite the island to the south of Morris Street, stretching all the way to Point Pleasant Park. The Deep Water piers could ultimately accommodate twenty-six vessels at a central location, with easy access and the magnificent ICR railway station close by on North Street. Cowie estimated it would cost $1.2 million per berth to expand the facility. Across the harbour at Tuft's Cove in Dartmouth, he thought it would be possible to build twenty-four berths. From his point of view, the chief disadvantage of Dartmouth was that it was too far from the city, and he gave other examples of port cities that had suffered disadvantages from erecting terminals too far from their centres: Quebec (Lévis), New York (Brooklyn), Liverpool (Birkenhead), London (Tilbury), and Montreal (Longueil). The estimated cost per berth at Tuft's Cove was $800,000. The third site examined was Dartmouth Cove, where a total of twenty-eight berths were possible at a cost of $880,000 each. The main disadvantage at this site was the height and steep slope of the land. Strangely, Cowie completely ignored the advantages of the area: rail access already running through the site and its close proximity to local factories such as Dartmouth Ropeworks, Starr Manufacturing, Acadia Sugar, and the refinery under construction at Imperoyal.

Cowie's preferred location, the one that was eventually chosen, was the George's Island Extension in the South End. The chief disadvantages of this site were the need for a railway cut passing through residential lands and its encroachment on Point Pleasant Park. The site was also more exposed to weather than the alternative at Deep Water Terminal.

ABOVE
Steele's Pond and the Greenbank area at Point Pleasant Park, with the future site of the Ocean Terminals in the background, circa 1888

OPPOSITE
A 1913 map in the Cowie Report showing the proposed Ocean Terminal sites

Cowie's vision for the site was truly breathtaking, even by today's standards. The total area to be developed was 260.5 acres, of which 198.5 were to be newly created land. The passenger landing quay was to be 2,006 feet (611 metres) long, with a shed 116 feet (35 metres) wide. The ground floor was to be used for freight and the second floor for passengers. Five additional piers and six basins 1,250 feet (380 metres) long and either 320 or 360 feet (98 or 110 metres) wide were to be built. A new freight yard was to be built between Rockingham and Fairview with material extracted from the railway cut. He also urged that a hotel be built adjacent to the main passenger terminal.

Cowie's plan was predicated on expanding markets and was not designed to take business away from other Canadian ports. This new business was to come from central and western Canada. From his perspective, it combined the best and most successful features of harbour design and the most up-to-date railway terminals. It was intended to serve entrepôt traffic, local commercial interests, and future business resulting from the establishment of new industries. Cowie alluded to an urgent requirement around the world "to increase the depth and dimensions of docks and piers." Experts were predicting the need for water depths of sixty feet (eighteen metres) in twenty to thirty years, and Cowie presciently recommended that Halifax

The groundbreaking for the new Ocean Terminals, July 31, 1913

A panoramic view of the Ocean Terminals construction site, 1914

not build anything less than forty-five feet (fourteen metres) in depth. The one glaring weakness in Cowie's report was the complete lack of economic analysis of the scheme and the site's total dependence on the port and railway to connect it to inland markets.

At first, there was some opposition to the plan from local residents, who feared the neighbourhood around the George's Island Extension site would be transformed from "a good residential, aristocratic district to a mechanic's district," but this was short-lived. Ultimately the project was heralded as "the complete triumph of progress."[47] As historian Jay White points out, "The port helped define the community's sense of identity" during this era, a statement that could be applied to many periods in the city's history.[48] Construction on the Ocean Terminals began in 1913, only to be interrupted in September 1914 by the declaration of war between Germany and Great Britain. By the time war was declared, only a small section had been completed, but work continued, albeit slowly, during the war.

Pier construction at the Ocean Terminals consisted of some twelve hundred concrete caissons, weighing 63 tons each, stacked on top of one another and reinforced with one thousand steel and concrete piles. Interior spaces were then filled with rubble stone. The concrete caissons were poured in a moulding yard on site, and over six hundred guide and key posts were fabricated at Eastern Passage and floated across the harbour. The massive enterprise of building

OPPOSITE
A granite-cutting shed and yard at the Ocean Terminals construction site, 1916

TOP LEFT
The construction site at Ocean Terminals with George's Island in the background, 1915

MIDDLE LEFT
The block-moulding yard at Ocean Terminals, 1915

BOTTOM LEFT
A section of the railway cut through the South End of Halifax leading to Ocean Terminals, 1915

Ocean Terminals also included blasting a new railway line through bedrock from Fairview in the North End to the terminal site in the South End, a distance of several kilometres. By 1916, about sixty-five percent of the railway cut had been completed.[49] About $7 million was expended on Ocean Terminals during the war, employing about nine hundred workers between 1915 and 1916. With all of the new infrastructure being built, the Port of Halifax seemed to be on the verge of greatness at last.

ss *Sheba*, shown here berthed along south wall of Pier A at Ocean Terminals, was the first vessel to arrive at the new docks, on November 7, 1916.

76 CANADA'S ATLANTIC GATEWAY

CHAPTER FOUR

The Great War
1914–1918

Like it had during the War of 1812 and the U.S. Civil War, the Port of Halifax proved its worth during the First World War. Despite the recession that had gripped the country in 1913, Halifax was a construction zone prior to the outbreak of the war in August 1914. Thomas Raddall estimated that almost $52 million in building permits had been issued in Halifax in 1913, including $35 million for a new railway terminal and station, $3.5 million for new railway piers at Deep Water Terminal, $170,000 for an extension to the Richmond railway docks, $1 million for the dry dock and shipbuilding plant at Halifax Industries, and another $1 million for fortifications and defence.[1] As well, a $3 million sugar refinery was under construction at Woodside across the harbour for the old Dartmouth enterprise Acadia Sugar, and a new Pier 2 at Deep Water Terminals had just been completed. It came none too soon, as the terminal handled 96,000 immigrants in 1913. After years of fighting for a more significant status in Canada, it finally seemed that Halifax was on its way to becoming Canada's eastern gateway.

The yard at Deep Water Terminal, circa 1912. The construction of new railway piers at Deep Water Terminal in Halifax's North End was one of many projects to receive government funds before the outbreak of the First World War.

Piers 2 and 3 at Deep Water Terminal, circa 1910

THE EARLY YEARS

War was thrust upon Halifax in August 1914, and Canada made an extraordinary contribution to the war effort. Out of a total population of some 5 million people, 500,000 men and women went overseas between 1914 and 1918, of whom an estimated 250,000 boarded their transports at Pier 2.[2] Unfortunately, over 50,000, or almost one percent of the country's population, never came home. On a per capita basis, it was one of the biggest Allied contributions to the war effort, along with those of Newfoundland (then a separate dominion) and Australia. This fact often gets overshadowed by the tragic events of the Halifax Explosion, and by the American contribution after the U.S. decided to enter the fray in April 1917.

Before the outbreak of the war, Canada's East Coast navy consisted of one meagre vessel, HMS *Niobe*, which was out of commission after having run aground while patrolling the South Shore of Nova Scotia. Canada faced the choice of either contributing money to the British Admiralty or building up its own navy. Wilfrid Laurier favoured the latter course, while Robert Borden, who won the federal election in 1911, wanted to provide three ships to the British Navy along with contributing to a common foreign policy for the empire. Borden's Naval Aid Bill was introduced in the House of Commons in December 1912 and passed in May 1913, but it was defeated in the Senate shortly thereafter. Borden gave up his quest, and in the meantime war intervened a year later. During the First World War, the role of Canada's navy, which consisted of a ragtag collection of what Raddall called "armed steamers, converted yachts, drifters, trawlers and motor boats," as well as tugboats and small steamers taken over from civilian departments, was to patrol the coast of Nova Scotia and keep the entrance to Halifax Harbour free of mines.[3] Over the course of the war, Canada's flotilla was expanded from about a dozen ships to over one hundred as a nascent shipbuilding industry sprung back into action. As well, the damages to HMS *Niobe* were repaired, and it rejoined the Canadian fleet in 1913.

Once again, the Port of Halifax became a Royal Navy base, and the British held sway over all vessel movements. As naval historian Roger Sarty writes, "the clock seemed to roll back to the 18th or early 19th century."[4] The old dockyard facilities established prior to the British departure in 1905 were just adequate for the ensuing task. The buildings were renumbered and some new ones were added. Wharf Number One was doubled in length and extended, creating

ABOVE
Canadian troops bound for Flanders wave a hearty goodbye as the camouflaged White Star liner *Olympic* prepares to leave Halifax, circa 1915.

FOLLOWING PAGE
HMS *Niobe* immobilized for repairs in a Halifax graving dock

a larger wharf capable of berthing vessels on both sides. Several workshops were also built for vessel repair and maintenance.[5]

As a defence, mines were laid across the entrance to the harbour between McNab's Island and Point Pleasant, leaving just a narrow channel for vessels to enter or leave. Two anti-submarine nets were strung from the Ocean Terminal breakwater to Ives Point and east and west from George's Island. As well, direction-finding stations were set up at Chebucto Head and elsewhere along the coast to assist in detecting German subs.

With the advent of war, port improvements were almost immediately curtailed, but sufficient progress had been made that the largest ships afloat, including *Olympic*, sister ship of the ill-fated *Titanic*, could dock at the new South End facilities without the aid of tugs by the end of 1916. However, most of the troopships, including *Olympic*, were usually handled at Deep Water Terminal.

CONVOYS

Although an ancient concept, the system of convoys to protect merchant shipping was not employed in the First World War until 1917, three years after the war began. Senior authorities in Britain thought convoys were obsolete in the age of steam.

TOP
A postcard view of Royal Navy vessels HMS *Pallas*, *Crescent*, *Diadem*, *Tribune*, *Psyche*, *Proserpine*, and *Indefatigable* in Halifax Harbour

ABOVE LEFT
Large ocean liners like *Olympic*, shown here at the coaling pier, could dock at the new Ocean Terminals by 1916.

ABOVE RIGHT
A ship laying electronically controlled mines in Halifax Harbour to protect against surface-borne raiders

ABOVE AND OPPOSITE
Scores of merchant vessels lie at anchor in Bedford Basin awaiting wartime sailing orders. Merchant ship losses dropped dramatically during both world wars with the implementation of the convoy system.

However, by the spring of 1917, one-quarter of all commercial vessels sailing across the Atlantic were being sunk, and it was clear that a new protection system was necessary. Shortly thereafter, the British Admiralty inaugurated a system of convoys that made extensive use of Halifax and other Canadian ports as dispatch points for ferrying goods, supplies, and soldiers to the front in Europe. German U-boats had much more difficulty finding thirty or forty vessels in a convoy than thirty or forty single sailings. Convoys could also be routed around areas where U-boats were known to be operating. Halifax, Sydney, Saint John, Quebec City, and Montreal became the principal departure ports of convoys supplying Britain.[6] Because of its importance as a dispatch point for convoys, the London *Times* called Halifax the "third most important port in the World."[7] Halifax's so-called handicap of geography—that is, the port's distance from major markets—had vanished, and it seemed clear to local promoters that what Halifax was accomplishing in wartime could be accomplished in peacetime. Sadly, port boosters would not have the opportunity to test this theory, as the Halifax Explosion on December 6, 1917, cut the port's run of prosperity short and unleashed unprecedented destruction on the city.

THE HALIFAX EXPLOSION

Nearly forty ships were at anchor in Bedford Basin awaiting the departure of two convoys in early December 1917. A schooner was loading lumber for the West Indies at Pier 6, and two British vessels were at Pier 8 loading horses. Another vessel, which had grounded off the coast, was waiting to unload its cargo of shells and grain at the refinery wharf prior to going into the dry dock next door. The Halifax Dockyard was full to brimming, and plans were afoot to take over the 900-foot (275-metre) sugar wharf when Acadia Sugar opened its new refinery in Woodside.[8]

On December 6, 1917, around 9:00 AM, the inbound French freighter *Mont Blanc*, filled with a lethal mix of 2,000 tons of explosives, including wet and dry picric acid, TNT, gun cotton, and benzene, collided with the outbound Norwegian steamer *Imo* in the narrows leading into Bedford Basin.[9] It was the largest human-made explosion of all time until the two atomic bombs were dropped on Nagasaki and Hiroshima in August 1945.

In the days prior to the explosion, *Mont Blanc* had loaded its cargo in New York, but it was too slow to join one of the fast twelve-to-thirteen-knot New York convoys. Instead, it had been ordered to Halifax to join a slower seven-to-eight-knot convoy. Upon the ship's arrival in Halifax at 4:30 PM on December 5, its captain was ordered to the Examination Anchorage just south

OPPOSITE
The billowing cloud from the Halifax Explosion

of Mauger's Beach. The anti-submarine gates to the harbour entrance were closed from dusk to dawn, so *Mont Blanc* was ordered to remain outside the harbour until sunrise.

Imo was a Norwegian vessel on charter to the Belgian Relief Commission. It had arrived in Halifax from Rotterdam on December 3, en route to New York to load relief supplies. It had been scheduled to leave on December 5 at 2:30 PM, but its coal tender had arrived too late to enable it to clear the harbour defences, so it was forced to lay at anchor another night in Bedford Basin. *Imo*'s captain was anxious to leave Halifax so as to clear the Nova Scotia coast and the danger of lurking submarines.

On the clear and crisp morning of December 6, *Mont Blanc* weighed anchor at 7:15 AM and was underway within fifteen minutes, proceeding through both sets of harbour defence nets. The vessel slowed to four knots to allow the Dartmouth ferry to pass, and continued at this speed towards the Narrows. Meanwhile, *Imo* got underway from its anchorage at 8:00 AM and sailed through a number of vessels in Bedford Basin before proceeding to the Narrows. As the ship reached the Narrows, the pilot noticed another vessel on the wrong side of the channel. Seeing this, *Imo*'s skipper, with the pilot's blessing, continued on his course along the Dartmouth shore and towards the inner harbour. At the same time, the pilot on board *Mont Blanc* noticed a vessel approaching his ship on the "wrong" side of the harbour. *Mont Blanc*'s captain signalled his intention to lay claim to that side of the channel, and *Imo*'s captain sent a similar signal signifying *his* intention to stay on his course. The two vessels were then on a collision course.

The ensuing explosion killed two thousand people, injured another nine thousand, and left twenty thousand homeless. It destroyed 320 acres of the city, including most of North End

THE GREAT WAR, 1914–1918 85

ABOVE
A train makes its way through the debris of what once was Pier 8 near ground zero in the aftermath of the Halifax Explosion.

OPPOSITE
While *Mont Blanc* virtually disintegrated in the explosion, *Imo*'s hull ended up on the Dartmouth shore.

Halifax, which included port facilities and many factories located at Richmond Terminals. Of the four piers located there, only Pier 9 was rebuilt and expanded. The explosion also destroyed the main rail line, the beautiful ICR train station, and the King Edward Hotel at North Street. Not a single building in the Halifax Dockyard was spared, either. Two buildings were destroyed completely and the rest were severely damaged.

In the aftermath of the explosion, on lands cleared by that unfortunate event, Halifax Shipyards Limited built a new steel shipbuilding plant just north of the dockyard, something that had been a civic obsession since at least 1898. The next year, it began turning out vessels

ABOVE
Although much of the dockyard was destroyed in the Halifax Explosion, more than thirty merchant vessels anchored in Bedford Basin survived with minimal damage, and the first post-explosion convoy sailed only four days later.

OPPOSITE
The Dominion Coal wharf at Pier 26, Ocean Terminals

of 8,390 and 10,500 tons displacement in response to a short-lived post-war boom in demand. The disaster also spurred on the construction of the Ocean Terminals in the South End, but it was not sufficient motivation to complete the project.

AFTERMATH

The war effort swelled port tonnage figures to unprecedented levels, from just over 2 million tons in 1913 to 17 million tons in 1917. The value of exports rose from $19 million in 1915 to $142 million two years later. In 1916, Imperial Oil began building an oil refinery along the Dartmouth shoreline, complete with its own company town, Imperoyal, but its construction was not finished until 1918, so it had little impact on wartime tonnage.

However, the conclusion of the war brought an end to the construction boom of the previous decade. With the election of William Lyon Mackenzie King and the Liberals in 1921, construction of port facilities, which had commenced in 1913 during Borden's Conservative regime and continued during the war, screeched to a halt. By this time, the facilities that had been completed at Ocean Terminals consisted of the 2,007-foot (610-metre) quay wall,

Basin #2 and the south wall of Pier A, Ocean Terminals

comprising berths 20–22, and Pier A, consisting of berths 23 to 28. At that time, Pier 26 was being leased to the Dominion Coal Company.[10]

The end of the First World War also brought with it a reorganization of Canada's transportation network, greatly affecting the status of the Port of Halifax. In 1918, the Canadian government took over majority ownership of the Canadian Northern Railway, which in turn was simultaneously taking control of the Canadian Government Railways (CGR), a group of railway companies including the old ICR, the National Transcontinental Railway (NTR), the Prince Edward Island Railway (PEIR), and several others. In order to streamline the operation and financial support of these various entities, the Canadian government merged them together as Canadian National Railways (CNR) shortly after their acquisition. By the early 1920s, both the Grand Trunk Pacific and the Grand Trunk had been folded into CNR, as well. At long last, Halifax finally had access to a true transcontinental railway system, like its rival Saint John already had with the CPR. Unfortunately, along with the restructuring of the railways came new policies, one of which stated that the ICR portion of the CNR would no longer have the ability to independently set lower rates to compensate for the fact that the line was not originally meant for commercial use. This new policy would have far-reaching consequences for the Maritime provinces.

CHAPTER FIVE

The Open Gateway
1919–1938

As many observers have noted, the Great Depression started early in the Maritimes, beginning shortly after the First World War. The Maritime Rights Movement of the 1920s was a reaction to the economic downturn the Maritime provinces were faced with after the war. According to its historian, Ernest R. Forbes, the Maritime Rights Movement was "a spontaneous expression of the social and economic frustration of the Maritime people," who were aggravated with their declining economy and political influence within Canada.[1] The Maritime industrial sector, which had already been struggling in the pre-war period, found itself severely challenged to compete with central Canadian companies in the post-war period. Some 1,100 Maritime firms disappeared in the 1920s, which led to substantial out-migration to Ontario, the Canadian West, and the "Boston States."

THE DUNCAN COMMISSION

Sir Andrew Rae Duncan, who headed up the Royal Commission on Maritime Claims in 1926 to address many of the issues raised by the Maritime Rights Movement, laid much of the blame for the region's plight on two fateful decisions. One related to the route that was chosen for the Intercolonial Railway, namely, "that strategic considerations determined the actual course of the line making it many miles longer than was necessary."[2] Sanford Fleming, its original surveyor, estimated that it was 250 miles (400 kilometres) longer than required if its purpose was to connect the Maritime provinces with the cities of the St. Lawrence. The other decision to negatively affect the economy of the region was "the extent that commercial considerations were subordinate to national, imperial and strategic considerations, the cost [for the ICR/CNR] would be borne by the Dominion and not by the traffic that might pass over the line."[3] With a few exceptions, most notably in regard to the sugar refining industry, this principle had been adhered to from 1876 to 1912. But from 1912 to 1926, in a move described by Forbes as "misguided symmetry," the cumulative increase of freight rates on the ICR/CNR amounted to 92 percent, whereas the rest of Canada endured increases in freight rates of "only" 55 percent.[4] These rate increases on freight being imported and exported to the Maritimes via the railways had a devastating effect on the regional economy.

HALIFAX HARBOUR COMMISSION

The Duncan Commission recommended several ways to improve the economy in the Maritimes, one of which involved the establishment of harbour commissions in Halifax and Saint John. Duncan reasoned that local interests would be better placed to guide port policy than federal bureaucrats. Thus, the Halifax Harbour Commission (HHC) was created in 1928, giving effective control of the port to the local community. The most important properties transferred to the HHC were the grain elevator owned by the Department of Trade and Commerce and other properties owned and operated by the Department of Railways, worth about $13 million in total. These included Richmond Terminals ($186,955), Deep Water Terminals ($1,508,134), and Ocean Terminals ($10,874,377), plus $529,712 for the cost of land.[5] A three-member board for the HHC was appointed on January 11, 1928, with Peter R. Jack as president. The commission was given wide-ranging powers to expropriate lands and administer the affairs of the port. It could also borrow money with the approval and guarantee of the federal government.

As of the HHC's inception in 1928, Halifax was a port of call for "most of the large cabin class passenger vessels en route from Europe to New York."[6] It was the Canadian port for regular cargo and passenger service, as well as coastal services for passengers and freight. Thirty-six passenger and freight services, as well as eight purely freight services, called at the port on a regular basis.

There were three main port facilities on the Halifax side of the harbour when the HHC took over control of the port: South Terminals, North Terminals, and Richmond Terminals.

A 1933 Halifax Harbour Commission debenture

The CNR and Dominion Atlantic Railway (the latter a subsidiary of the CPR) had rail facilities at the South and North terminal wharves. The port also boasted a large dry dock facility, which employed two thousand people at its peak in 1918.[7] It covered 46 acres along the waterfront from the north side of the dockyard to Richmond Terminal. Imperoyal, on the Dartmouth side of the harbour, was the largest oil refinery in Canada and covered some 142 acres. It fell outside the HHC's jurisdiction, but contributed substantially to the port's overall cargo tonnage. The port's cargo handling was performed by residents of Halifax and surrounding towns and villages, and was notable for being largely exempt from labour disputes because the workers were mostly seasonal and casual.

As soon as it was appointed, the HHC set about extending and expanding the port's facilities. It proposed to spend $10 million on an ambitious variety of projects, including an extension to Pier 9 and the construction of a new reinforcing wall at Deep Water Terminals, Marginal Road, sheds 23 to 26, two transit sheds at Pier A, three transit sheds at Pier B, a new pier at Pier B, and a grain elevator and grain jetty.[8]

The HHC subsequently undertook to finally complete the Ocean Terminals, starting with Pier 21 in 1928 and Pier B in 1930. The original plan called for Piers C, D, and E, but they were never built. It also followed up a recommendation of the Duncan Commission with the construction of Public Cold Storage Terminals Ltd., a cold storage plant at Pier 26, which was a unique public and private investment. The idea was to encourage the shipment of local fish and produce through local ports and to serve as a local distribution centre for fresh produce. The owners of the plant, including W. A. Black, Cyril W. Stairs, Ralph Bell, and several other prominent Haligonians, were given a 99-year lease on 7.25 acres of port land. The facility opened in

A 1928 Halifax Harbour Commission map showing the locations of various docks, terminals, and facilities

May 1929 after an investment of $2,250,000. However, the company ran into financial difficulties a few years later, and in 1933 it was bought out by the HHC for $1.7 million, ending the public-private partnership experiment.

The HHC's first annual report, published in 1929, describes the new projects that the commission had underway at the time, including Terminal Road; Shed 20 and port administration offices; Shed 27 and an adjoining shed; and an extension of the recently built grain elevator, including new dock spout grain towers, a car dumper in the unloading house, and an extension of its galleries and conveyors. The renovations doubled the elevator's capacity, and grain shipments increased from 2.7 million bushels in 1928 to 7.2 million in 1929. Total tonnage across all HHC facilities in 1929 was 328,925 tons of imports and 561,743 tons of exports, for a total of 600,688 tons. Total port traffic was estimated at 1,850,000 tons, up 27 percent from

the 1,450,000 tons the previous year. It appeared that Duncan's prediction that local interests would serve the port better than federal bureaucrats was correct. The HHC's investment in port infrastructure was paying off, and port traffic seemed to be on the rise once again.

THE LADY BOATS

Increased trade between Halifax and the Caribbean, spurred on by the foundation of a new CN shipping line, also helped to boost port traffic in the inter-war years. In December 1928, two years after a trade agreement was signed between Canada and Jamaica, CN Steamships introduced a new shipping service sailing out of Montreal, Halifax, and Saint John, serving Demerara, Guyana, as well as Bermuda, the Bahamas, and Jamaica, using five purpose-built vessels. These beautiful white "Lady Boats," as they became known, were built with $10 million in federal assistance, and were named after the wives of British admirals: Nelson, Drake, Hawkins, Rodney, and Somers. They carried passengers, sugar, bananas, and mail between Canada and the Caribbean.[9] According to Felicity Hanington, *Lady Rodney* and *Lady Somers* "sailed from Halifax in winter and Montreal in summer, taking a month to complete a cruise to Bermuda, Nassau and Jamaica."[10] The whole cruise cost $95. *Lady Nelson*, *Lady Drake*, and *Lady Hawkins*, each of which had accommodations for 338 passengers and 270,000 cubic feet of cargo, operated on a year-round eastern itinerary that included Halifax, Bermuda, St. Kitts, Nevis, Antigua, Montserrat, Dominica, St. Lucia, Barbados, St. Vincent, Grenada, Trinidad, and Demerara, returning via the same route to Saint John. The western itinerary included Montreal (in summer), Bermuda, Nassau, Kingston, and Halifax (in winter). The vessels on this route, *Lady Rodney* and *Lady Somers*, had accommodations for just 130 first-class passengers and

ABOVE
Pier B, circa 1935

TOP
The cold storage plant at Pier 26

OPPOSITE
A locomotive makes its way through Ocean Terminals

THE OPEN GATEWAY, 1919–1938   97

328,000 cubic feet of cargo. The Lady Boats remained in service until the Second World War, when they were requisitioned for war service. *Lady Somers*, *Lady Hawkins*, and *Lady Drake* were subsequently torpedoed and sunk, while *Lady Nelson* and *Lady Rodney* were damaged but later repaired. The two remaining Lady Boats resumed service from Halifax and Montreal after the war in 1947, sailing the Caribbean route until 1952, when they were sold.

ABOVE
Lady Nelson

OPPOSITE
The construction of Shed 20 and the port administration offices

PIER 21

Pier 21, Halifax's new immigration shed, also had a positive effect on port traffic in the interwar years. The facility opened on March 28, 1928, heralding a new era that saw Halifax become the primary entry point for immigrants entering Canada. The two-storey, 600-foot-long (183-metre-long) facility was immense, covering 221,000 square feet (20,500 square metres). It was connected to an immigration annex and the CN passenger station. The first floor handled freight and the second floor held what authors Alexa Thompson and Debi van de Wiel describe as "a reception area for immigrants, a medical clinic, complete with hospital and waiting rooms for those requiring medical examinations, kitchens, cafeterias and a canteen."[11] There was a nursery and dormitory for up to 150 people, as well as a detention centre. In its first few years of operation, Pier 21 handled about 45,000 people per annum. However, this quickly dropped off to around 20,000 immigrants per year in 1930 and fell below 3,000 per year as the Depression deepened.

PORT DEVELOPMENT

Notwithstanding the depressed state of the world economy in early 1930, the Halifax Harbour Commission made a proposal to the minister of marine and fisheries for an aggressive port development program. The proposed plan was "for all intents and purposes" the completion of the original Ocean Terminal scheme begun by the Department of Railways in 1913.[12] The HHC believed that Halifax had much unfulfilled potential if only (1) Canadian cargo (i.e. grain) moved through Canadian ports, (2) British preferential tariffs restricted such cargo to Canadian ports, and (3) immigrants were encouraged to pass through Canadian ports.

ABOVE
The Red Cross canteen at Pier 21, circa 1930

TOP
Immigrant children in the Red Cross nursery at Pier 21

OPPOSITE
The Red Cross nursery at Pier 21, circa 1930

ABOVE
The second-floor immigration reception area at Pier 21

The HHC maintained that its facilities were actually congested at certain times of the year. On winter weekends, for example, it had to accommodate 20 to 26 vessels and had only 14 berths to do it. By this time, the port had 48 shipping lines using its facilities, including coastal services. Around 1,600 steamers used the port in 1929, compared with 1,525 the previous year. These included *Kungsholm* of the Swedish-America Line, *St. Louis* of the Hamburg-America Line,[13] *Minnewaska* of the American Transport Lines, and *Carmania* of the Cunard Line. The HHC was also expecting an increase in traffic in the following year.

The HHC told the minister that the port had lost business due to insufficient facilities. The commissioners also complained that Canadian cargo made up eighty-five percent of New York's export grain shipments and twenty percent of its total export shipments, and argued that Canadian grain should be shipped out of Canadian ports. A follow-up sent to the deputy minister made the argument that "it has been proved by the experience of ports all over the world that facilities must be provided ahead of actual demand if the business of the port is to progress."[14]

Unfortunately, the HHC's proposal was destined to come to naught. The federal election of 1930 saw Richard B. Bennett and the Conservatives assume power from Mackenzie King and the Liberals, and the HHC, which had been appointed by the Liberals, was about to undergo some drastic changes as a result.

A NEW REGIME

On July 28, 1930, Prime Minister Bennett's Conservative broom swept the Halifax Harbour Commission clean. Peter Jack, who had run for the Liberals and lost, resigned as chairman, to be replaced in the interim by C. W. Ackhurst. In September 1930, a new board consisting of E. C. Phinney, J. L. Hetherington, and F. P. Merchant was named. An employment office was opened within weeks of their appointment, as was a port traffic department. In early October, the HHC chauffeur was dismissed, as were seven members of the HHC fire brigade, presumably because of their affiliations with the Liberals. Soon afterwards, in November 1930, an inquiry led by Justice John F. Orde was appointed to investigate the affairs of the previous administration, which was accused of having issued "improvident contracts" and exercising partisan influence over the former commission's affairs.[16] The allegations were never proven, and Orde died before his report was issued.

The new HHC board members were quick to put their stamp on the organization. Twenty-one appointments were made to the commission's police force in November 1930. Work rules were issued around the same time, prohibiting smoking in general offices and all corridors. The daily lunch break was changed to one-and-a-half hours, and office hours were restricted to 9:00 AM to 5:30 PM. The board members also expanded the HHC by hiring a number of new employees; by January 1931, the HHC employed 155 people.

E. C. Phinney, president of the Halifax Harbour Commission, 1930–33

THE DEPRESSION

At the same time that the HHC was undergoing its transformation, port traffic was beginning to feel the effects of the Depression. Total tonnage over HHC wharves in 1930 was down about 11 percent over the previous year, to 799,272 tons. Total port traffic for the year was estimated to be 1,825,000 tons (the additional 1 million tons over the HHC wharf numbers was handled at private facilities located within the port, including the Imperial Oil refinery at Imperoyal). Canadian grain was still moving over U.S. ports, but the HHC's new traffic department had managed to negotiate for cargoes of export seed and potatoes and import fruits and vegetables from the British West Indies.

Shortly thereafter, E. C. Phinney initiated discussions with the Saint John Harbour Commission to discuss matters of "mutual interest." He also restated the longstanding desire to bring the CPR to Halifax, arguing that it was "absolutely essential to have competition by the Railways."[17] As well, the port's management travelled to Winnipeg and, together with the Maritime Board of Trade, applied for the publication of an all-rail rate on grain in carloads from Armstrong, Port Arthur, and Westford, Ontario, travelling over the National Transcontinental route to Saint John, West Saint John, and Halifax. The appeal was dismissed. The port again suffered another decline in cargo, from 799,272 tons in 1930 to 701,997 in 1931. The only increases came in agricultural exports, while the biggest decline came in transatlantic cargo. Port tonnage as a whole was down to 1.5 million tons by the end of 1931.

The HHC's new management made a genuine effort to promote the interests of the port. The magazine *Open Gateway*, extolling the virtues of the Port of Halifax, was published monthly. The HHC's own advertising campaign emphasized the straight, wide, deep channel, its easy access,

J. L. Hetherington, the third president of the Halifax Harbour Commission, 1933–35

and the infrequent need for tugs to assist in docking large vessels. A constant theme was that the port was "always open to all shipping."[18]

Another of management's undertakings was to meet with members of the local shipping community to discuss various issues. This was undoubtedly a good idea, since there were still about thirty-six private wharves and piers that were in many respects competing with public facilities. As well, in anticipation of Sir Alexander Gibb's visit to Halifax to examine the administration of the harbour, the commission met with the Halifax Board of Trade's transportation committee, which, it acknowledged, had "for so long carried out some of the functions of the HHC."

THE GIBB REPORT

Sir Alexander Gibb was originally appointed to examine the administration of harbours in Montreal, Vancouver, Quebec, Halifax, and Saint John. He also carried out "subsidiary" investigations in New Westminster, Victoria, Fort William, Port Arthur, Trois-Rivières, and Chicoutimi. His mandate was to determine the best method of administering Canadian ports, to evaluate the relationship between existing facilities and future requirements, and to make recommendations regarding the nature and scope of development for each port for the next twenty-five to fifty years. In this respect, Gibb addressed concerns that commission ports had overspent and over-expanded in the brief period they had been in existence.

When they met with Gibb, the HHC had a blunt message for him. One of the basic premises of Confederation had been to provide Canada with a year-round outlet to the sea. The transcontinental railways and the east-west national policy had been developed in

Entrance to the Port of Halifax, the "Open Gateway," circa 1930s

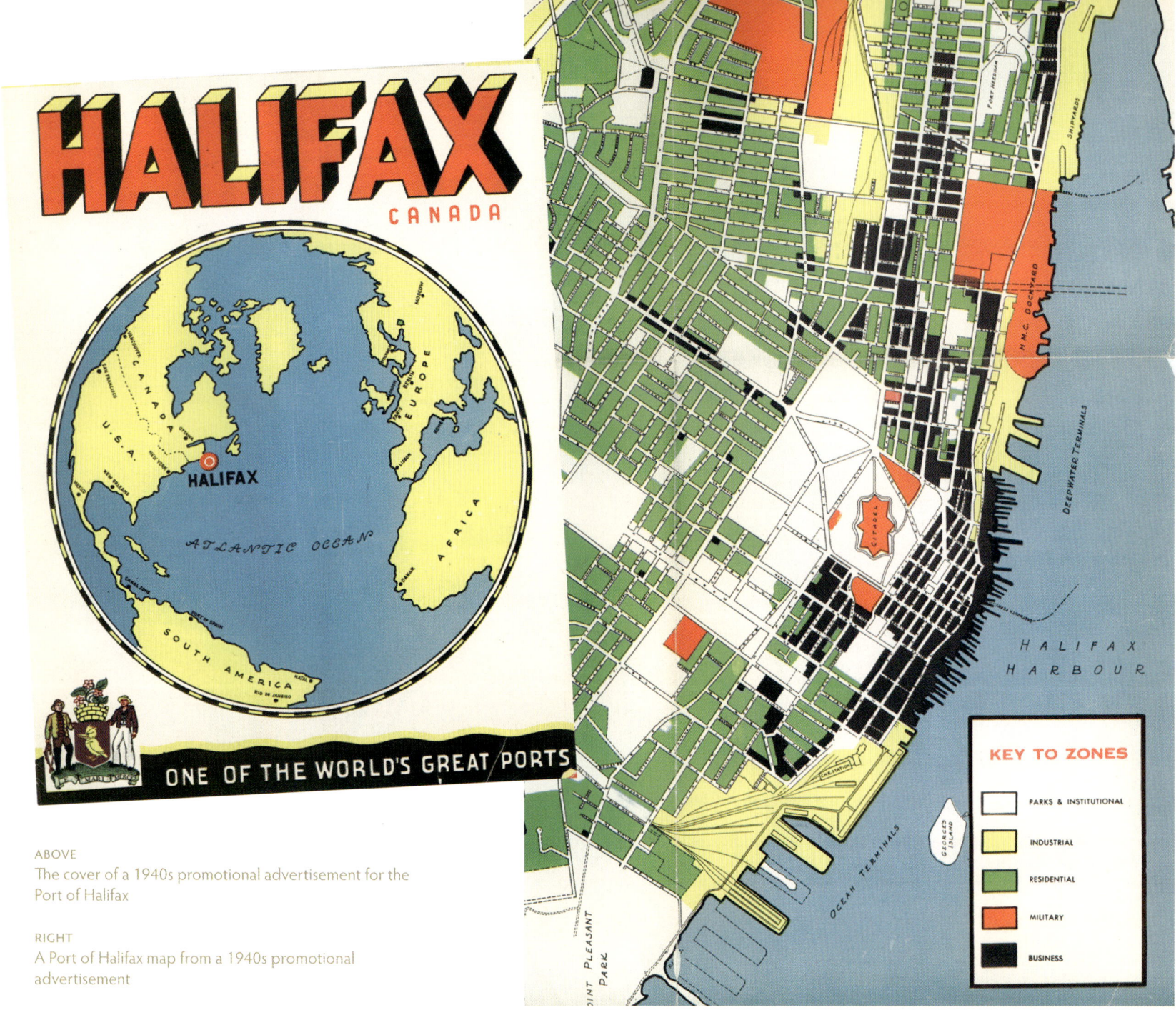

ABOVE
The cover of a 1940s promotional advertisement for the Port of Halifax

RIGHT
A Port of Halifax map from a 1940s promotional advertisement

support of this notion, but the HHC contended that the practice in the intervening years had been "inimical" to this policy, with Montreal interests playing off the summer traffic in American grain against the winter movement of Canadian grain. The HHC told Gibb that Canada "must decide whether she is going to develop her Atlantic ports or whether to shut them down."[19] At the same meeting, they also discussed the issue of CPR running rights, as well as a very intriguing idea to "take back" the ICR from CN and allow both railways to operate on the same track. The HHC's submission summarized the development of the Port of Halifax from Confederation. At the outset, the commissioners stated their support for the Duncan Commission's recommendation that ports be administered locally. They also reiterated a longstanding Halifax complaint regarding the inefficient routing of the ICR/CNR. In addition, they argued that the port needed new infrastructure to relieve some of the congestion at its facilities.

Halifax's facilities were quite intensively used by this time. Pier 9 was used for bulk cargo such as coal, fertilizer, cement, and petroleum, as well as full cargoes of lumber and cattle. Deep Water Terminal handled potatoes from PEI, lumber, and general cargo. Piers 23 and 25 at Ocean Terminals handled general cargo and the coastwise trade, as well as vessels from the West Indies, Australia, New Zealand, and South America. Pier 24 handled full cargoes of perishables such as potatoes and turnips bound for the West Indies, Cuba, and certain U.S. destinations. The grain elevator handled import and coastwise grain shipments.

Halifax basically functioned as a "port of call" for transatlantic vessels; vessels called at Halifax on the way to or from another port, usually New York, but most did not use Halifax as a home port and did not undertake full discharges or load operations at the port. Halifax's

ABOVE
The grain galleries at Ocean Terminals, 1929

OPPOSITE
The grain elevator at Ocean Terminals, 1929

berth operation, or density, was of a much different ratio as compared to ports where shipping companies had home port operations. In order to become more than a port of call, Halifax would have to develop so-called ballast cargoes, the best of which was grain. The commission argued that Halifax's grain-handling capacity of about fifteen million bushels was being underutilized. To achieve maximum capacity, they would require an adjustment in rail rates. They also suggested that furtherance rates for traffic to Newfoundland could be adjusted and that the government examine the possibility of pro-rating revenues via strategic gateways.

One of the recommendations of the commissioners would have had far-reaching consequences for the city had it been acted upon. Because of the cost of switching cargoes between Deep Water Terminal and Ocean Terminals, with the additional distance of eight miles (thirteen kilometres) via Rockingham, the commissioners advocated a direct rail connection along the waterfront, a distance of just one mile (just over one-and-a-half kilometres). In

ABOVE
Imperial Oil Refinery, Imperoyal, Dartmouth

OPPOSITE
Acadia Sugar Refinery, Dartmouth

effect, the commission wanted to take over the whole downtown waterfront, which would have added at least sixty acres to their total land area. They also envisioned moving the navy to Dartmouth and taking over the Halifax Dockyard as well as completing Piers A and B at Ocean Terminals. If traffic warranted, they planned to revive the scheme Frederick Cowie had rejected before the First World War to build a terminal in Dartmouth Cove.

The Gibb Report of 1933 pointed out a seeming contradiction between national policy and reality. The country was predicated on the development of an east-west economy, but much to the chagrin of the "seaboard provinces," only fifty-two percent of Canada's eastern exports moved via Canadian ports in 1931. Gibb disagreed with the commissioners' claim that Halifax was congested. He saw little evidence of this. He also pointed out that only one-half of the port's cargo moved over HHC wharves, with the crude and refined oil handled at Imperoyal, sugar at Acadia Sugar in Woodside, and coal at Cunard Wharf. Gibb concluded with a very sobering message: "The possession of the finest harbour in Canada is not sufficient alone to make Halifax into a great port. In certain ways it is handicapped to an extent that largely offsets its natural advantages, and it will only attain an important future by constant effort and enterprise."[20]

Gibb agreed that Halifax should be served by the CPR, "as terminals of the Intercolonial and [National] Transcontinental Railways, built as national enterprises with national funds should be served equally and unrestrictedly by both railways."[21] He did not think Halifax's future depended on securing long-distance heavy freight "with abnormal reductions in rail rates," nor did he agree with the commission's assertion that Halifax would get a proportionate increase in cargo handled at Canadian ports. Instead, he suggested that the port concentrate on a number of priorities, including large vessels, the quickest passenger link to Europe, "high class fast freight," passenger traffic in winter, and trade between Canada and Newfoundland, the West Indies, and South America. According to Gibb, the port's hinterland potential was "not very considerable," its population growth was very slow, and its industrial enterprises were not close enough to the end consumer due to the length of the rail haul. He was, however, impressed with Halifax's potential to develop as a redistribution centre, or entrepôt, which would expand the port's potential hinterland. Gibb suggested that such a facility could be built by private interests or the port itself, and recommended that a warehouse be built in the most expedient fashion.

Gibb thought Halifax should establish itself as a first-class passenger port, especially for the winter months. He pointed out that the largest passenger vessels in the world could berth there. He also saw some potential for mail service and sea-air links for high-class package freight. In terms of facilities, he thought Halifax would be well endowed with cargo facilities once Pier B was completed, giving the port thirteen full-sized berths. He did not think the existence of the framework of a berth south of Pier A should be used as an argument to go ahead with the early construction of a pier there. He argued that the priority should be placed on obtaining better utilization of the Deep Water Terminal for freight liners and general cargo, rather than on expanding Ocean Terminals.

In retrospect, Gibb thought it had been a mistake to build Ocean Terminals in the South End because there was little interconnectivity between that site and the Halifax Harbour Commission docks further north. On that basis he agreed with the idea to build a railway between Deep Water Terminal and Ocean Terminals. But he thought the commission was dreaming when it envisaged taking over the whole shoreline, including the shipyard, the naval dockyard, and the downtown waterfront, saying traffic levels could not justify it for at least another twenty-five years. However, he did recommend that the commission secure those properties if they were to become available.

Gibb made three principal recommendations in his report: (1) that port development and administration for all Canadian ports should be centralized in Ottawa, (2) that port managers should be appointed by a central board, and (3) that local advisory councils should be established to provide local input.[22] His recommendations were not acted upon until after the Liberals were returned to power in 1935, whereupon the new minister of industry, C. D. Howe, oversaw the creation of the National Harbours Board (NHB) in 1936. The federal government assumed responsibility for eight ports nationwide, and from this point until the 1990s all major decisions affecting Canada's ports had to be vetted by a central bureaucracy in Ottawa. This new policy was not particularly popular in Halifax.

Pier A and Shed 28, with Shed 27 under construction in the background, Ocean Terminals, 1929

PORT CARGO

In the meantime, the HHC's share of port traffic declined 3.3 percent, from 701,998 tons in 1931 to 678,827 tons in 1932. Traffic in the port as a whole was also down 8.3 percent, from 1,591,066 tons in 1931 to 1,458,083 tons in 1932. The private terminals shared in the decline, down 12.3 percent from 889,068 tons to 779,256 tons. However, it appeared that some of the HHC's tactics to promote the port were paying off, as passenger traffic totalled 58,238 in 1932, up 4.7 percent from 55,598 in 1931, and the message regarding grain shipments was getting through, with an increase from 2.3 million bushels to more than 4.2 million bushels. Interestingly, the HHC's annual report introduced a new measure, "berth density," which it pegged at 61.5 percent in 1931 and 63.2 percent in 1932, noting that vessels were bunched at weekends, especially in winter.

The following year showed an improvement. The HHC had a profit of $59,747, of which $52,064 was transferred to the Department of Public Works; the commission still had a deficit of $273,000, brought forward from previous years. Cargo increased 25 percent, to 853,053 tons, largely on the basis of increases in agricultural products, mainly wheat and apples. The port also deployed its new marine leg, handling its first shipment of water-borne grain for domestic use. The best-performing trade routes were the transatlantic, St. Lawrence–Great Lakes, and Asia routes. New

ABOVE
The Bayers Road Bridge
(ocean side), 1918

LEFT
Ocean Terminals and the Hotel Nova
Scotian (now the Westin Nova Scotian)
as viewed from the southwest

services visiting the port in 1933 included the American Hampton Roads Line and the American Manchurian Line.

THE PORT AND THE CITY

Developments in the Port of Halifax throughout the inter-war years caused the city's appearance to change dramatically. The railway cut was completed, Ocean Terminals and the CN-owned Hotel Nova Scotian (now the Westin Nova Scotian) were built, and Pleasant Street disappeared. In 1934, Prime Minister Bennett opened Pier B with much fanfare. There was a transformation in the North End, as well, with the reconstruction of Richmond Terminal. The Department of National Defence also contributed to the city's changing appearance with the construction of a new ammunition magazine on the eastern slope of Bedford Basin. Thomas Raddall thought it an odd choice, commenting: "Many a tourist regarding the idyllic scene across the water from the train or a car on the Bedford highway must have wondered what unromantic architect had designed the grim 'houses' that looked out on such a view."[23]

By 1938, Halifax had once again closed the gap between itself and Saint John, and now boasted more berthing space than its rival across the Bay of Fundy; indeed, the port was second only to Montreal when it came to berthing space. At this point, the largest firms on the water-

ABOVE
A postcard view showing Piers 19 to 21 with the Nova Scotia Light and Power plant at the far left and numerous tramcar sheds immediately adjacent. The stately Hotel Nova Scotian and the attached Canadian National Railway Terminus, both of which opened in 1930, appear at right, foreground.

OPPOSITE
The Cunard liner *Queen Mary* at Halifax, circa 1930s

front were Canadian National Steamships, Cunard White Star Line, Furness Withy & Co. Ltd., A. G. Jones and Company, T. A. S. DeWolfe & Sons, Ltd., Pickford and Black, I. H. Mathers & Son, Scotia Stevedoring Co. Ltd., F. K. Warren, and Newfoundland-Canada Steamships Ltd.[24]

In spite of all this progress, Halifax's comparative lack of stature in the shipping world was unfortunately symbolized by the decision of the Cunard Line to bypass its spiritual home port when it launched the original *Queen Mary* in 1934. But with another world war looming, the Port of Halifax would see its stature in both the shipping and military worlds rise up once again.

CHAPTER SIX

Halifax and the Battle of the Atlantic
1939–1945

Halifax played a pivotal role in the Second World War. It was a major convoy assembly port, and it served as the primary base for the Canadian navy, a repair centre for damaged merchant ships, a refuelling base for Allied ships, and an embarkation point for soldiers going overseas.[1] It also continued to serve as a commercial port.

Halifax's role in the Second World War was crucial to keeping supply lines open and sustaining the war effort. Initially, Halifax was a Royal Navy port. In 1941, the U.S. navy took over control of naval operations in the Atlantic theatre. In 1943, the Royal Canadian Navy (RCN) assumed this responsibility.[2] By then, the RCN had grown from a peacetime force of 1,800 to a company of over 75,000 men and women, of whom 17,000 were stationed in Halifax by the war's end.

The Battle of the Atlantic was the longest battle of the Second World War, and "the most complex submarine war in history," in the words of author Marc Milner.[3] It began on September 3,

Batteries of twin-barrel rapid-fire guns such as the one pictured here, circa early 1940s, deterred speedy torpedo boats from reaching harbour approaches.

1939, when a German U-boat sank the unarmed liner *Athenia* 200 miles (320 kilometres) off the coast of the Hebrides in Scotland. Sailing from Liverpool to Montreal, *Athenia* had been carrying 1,400 passengers aboard. Shortly after the *Athenia* incident, shipping control authorities at Canadian ports ordered all shipping to Halifax, which the Admiralty had selected as the main assembly point for convoys sailing from North America to Great Britain. In Halifax, as Thomas Raddall relates, "batteries of anti-aircraft guns and searchlights sprang up like a fairy toadstool ring in the wooded hills around the port, and were placed on the roofs of downtown stores and elsewhere in the city."[4] Through the months of November and December of 1939, workers installed an anti-submarine net between Mauger's Beach on McNab's Island and York Redoubt on the south mainland. Costing some $300,000, it was made of steel cable and supported by buoys. The entrance to the harbour was also guarded by two gate ships, one painted red and the other painted green.

TOP
Banks of search lights at York Redoubt, circa early 1940s

BOTTOM
The anti-submarine net strung between McNab's Island and York Redoubt and the vessels guarding the harbour entrance, circa early 1940s

CONVOYS

Having learned a valuable lesson in the First World War, when the Royal Navy had been reluctant to introduce a convoy system to protect merchant and naval ships from German U-boats, Britain fully embraced convoys in the Second World War. About 500,000 men and women passed through Halifax on their way to the front in 150 troop convoys, which used the rail yard and the large sheds at Ocean Terminals in the South End to convene. Troops were transported to the front on ships of all sizes.

Convoys were used to protect merchant shipping, as well. The first Atlantic shipping convoy sailed from Britain just four days after the conflict started in September 1939 and the last sailed in May 1945, just after Victory in Europe Day. Only vessels that could make better than fifteen knots were allowed to sail independently. Those that made less than nine knots were placed in "slow" convoys sailing out of Sydney, and those that could do between nine and fifteen knots were placed in "fast" convoys sailing from Halifax. The slow convoys were obviously the most vulnerable, and they consisted of some of the oldest and creakiest vessels in the North Atlantic, most of which had been pressed into wartime duty to carry grain and timber. In 1941, HX (Halifax) convoys sailed every six days. Combined with the SC (Sydney) convoys, there were four sailings every twelve days, two from each harbour. As well, with upwards of one hundred German subs in the North Atlantic (forty-five on patrol and sixty heading to and from operational areas) and attacks becoming more prevalent, coastal convoys became necessary, with the first sailing in January 1942.

At their peak in 1943, there were 230 German U-boats harassing Allied ships in the North Atlantic. However, as Roger Sarty argues, "the combination of support groups, strengthened air cover and timely Ultra intelligence swung the balance decisively against the U-boats" in the first three weeks of May 1943, when 30 submarines were destroyed in exchange for the sinking of "only" 50 merchant vessels.[5] As Sarty points out, "more was at stake [in the Battle of the Atlantic] than Britain's war effort." The Allies' plans for landing in northwest Europe hinged on

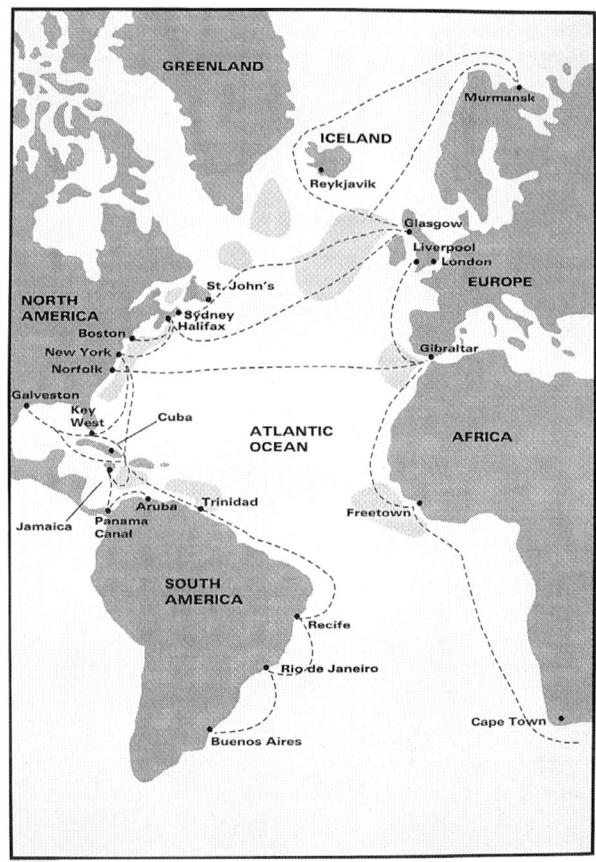

A map of Second World War convoy routes

TOP
Canadian troops bound for England depart Halifax from Pier 21, circa early 1940s

BOTTOM
Two luxury liners filled to capacity with Canadian troops await orders to leave Halifax, circa early 1940s

the outcome of the Battle of the Atlantic. If merchant shipping losses had continued unabated in the early 1940s, it would not have been possible to build up the hundreds of thousands of troops and the millions of tons of equipment needed to mount the invasion of Normandy in June 1944.

Between 1939 and 1945, 1,468 convoys crossed the North Atlantic. A typical convoy consisted of thirty-two merchant vessels escorted by two destroyers and four corvettes, which were stationed around the convoy. In late 1941, the Americans joined the war effort and took charge of the Atlantic area west of Iceland, allowing the British to concentrate on the eastern Atlantic. From then on, ships sailed from Halifax and joined up with either the Boston or New York convoys in mid-ocean. The largest convoy to sail during the Second World War was HXS 300, originating in New York on July 17, 1944, and consisting of 167 ships carrying over a million tons of cargo. This particular convoy was escorted by an RCN frigate and six corvettes, without a single ship lost.

At the start of the war, Canada's fleet could best be described as "modest," consisting of just one flotilla of destroyers and a single squadron of flying boats. The country had a meagre merchant fleet, as well. Yet by 1942, as Roger Sarty writes, "Canada was one of the foremost Allied powers in the Battle of the Atlantic," with over 95,000 personnel, including 6,000 women.[6] Canada built 500 combat vessels and another 410 cargo vessels in the short span of less than six years. At the beginning of the war, there were 3,600 people working in the country's shipyards; at the end, there were over 125,000.

Canada's role in the Battle of the Atlantic had been to protect Allied shipping and the supply lines to Britain. There were 25,343 merchant ship voyages between North America and Britain during the Second World War, carrying 164,783,921 tons of cargo, all of which were under Canadian escort. While undertaking these dangerous missions, Canadian warships and aircraft sank fifty German U-boats.[7] Unfortunately, these missions brought about losses on the Canadian side, as well. In total, the Royal Canadian Navy lost 2,024 personnel in the Battle of the Atlantic and the Royal Canadian Air Force lost 752 in maritime operations.

A flotilla of destroyers lies alongside Jetty No. 4 at HMC Dockyard, with merchant vessels riding anchor in Halifax Harbour in the background, May 1941

PORT ACTIVITY

Halifax's importance as a naval shore establishment during the Battle of the Atlantic cannot be underestimated. Notwithstanding its use as a convoy assembly point, its most valuable function was that of a repair and maintenance facility for merchant and naval vessels. At the beginning of the war, there was some thought given to creating a world-class repair base in the city, but the idea was abandoned for being too costly. Instead, a 24,000-ton floating dry dock was built and installed at Halifax Shipyards in 1942. From 1939 to 1945, 7,145 vessels were repaired at facilities in Halifax.[8]

As might be expected, there was a shipping boom during the Second World War, and

RIGHT
Hundreds of corvettes such as the one pictured here, circa early 1940s, were built during the Second World War for use by the Canadian Navy.

OPPOSITE TOP
SS *Marquesa* at the floating dry dock in Halifax, circa early 1940s

OPPOSITE BOTTOM
Changing shifts at the dockyard, circa early 1940s

several other wartime capital projects were undertaken to enhance the port's facilities and capabilities. The period between 1941 and 1942 was the busiest time for commercial shipping, with as many as 150 merchant ships in port at one time. In 1943, U.S. ports began to be used for wartime shipping and Halifax port traffic was somewhat reduced. From the beginning of the war to the end, over 27,000 vessels sailed in and out of Halifax, and from 1940 to 1945, the National Harbours Board facilities in Halifax handled 31.9 million tons of cargo.

One of the most unusual visitors to the port during the war was the 80-ton motor schooner *St. Roch*, which arrived in October 1942.[9] *St. Roch* was the second ship to make it through the mythical Northwest Passage, but the first to travel the passage from west to east, a voyage that took twenty-eight months, starting in October 1940. In 1944, it returned to Vancouver via the more northerly route of the Northwest Passage, making the run in eighty-six days. *St. Roch* was, in effect, a floating detachment of the Royal Canadian Mounted Police, under whose command the vessel was operated. In the ten years prior to the war, it had functioned as an Arctic patrol and supply ship. But during the war, the voyages of *St. Roch* through the

Northwest Passage helped establish Canadian sovereignty in the Arctic, and extended Canadian control over its vast northern territories.[10] Retired after returning from the Arctic in 1948, the vessel was sent back to Halifax by way of the Panama Canal in 1950, making it the first ship to circumnavigate North America.

CARGO-HANDLING AND WARTIME LABOUR

Wartime Halifax was a raucous, crowded, and sometimes unpleasant place to be. During the war, the population on the peninsula increased by 30,000, or about 50 percent, over the pre-war figure, a huge addition by any measure. Most of the influx was due to workers moving to Halifax to gain employment in wartime enterprises. One of the key activities in Halifax during the war was loading and unloading ships for the convoys. The port's cargo-handling facilities were quite substantial by the outset of the war, amounting to three miles (nearly five kilometres) of berths, thirteen transit sheds, a cold storage shed, and a large grain elevator. However, one serious deficiency in port functionality was in the way ship loading was handled.

Until 1939, dockside labour had been controlled by the

major shipping agencies and stevedoring companies. Men were hired in the morning and let go when the job was finished. "Dockworkers did not know from one day to the next whether they would be employed, and few could make a living strictly from stevedoring," Jay White explains.[11] Waterfront work was a casual and secondary occupation, often performed by farmers and fishermen because most of the work was only available in the winter. There was, however, a union, Local 269 of the International Longshoremen's Association (ILA), which represented a small group of permanent longshore labourers that had first rights of refusal at whatever work was available.

By the fall of 1940, with the increased number of convoys requiring faster turnarounds, it became apparent that the peacetime labour-management structure and the method of dockside operations were too inefficient. In January 1941, the ILA agreed to admit 200 "temporary" members to the union, who would have no right to union benefits. But it soon became apparent that round-the-clock loading and unloading operations were necessary, and the federal government passed an Order-in-Council to allow as many "card men" (casual workers) as required to handle the extra traffic. By the end of 1941, 2,700 stevedores were employed at Halifax, of whom 900 were members of the ILA, 650 were card men, and the rest were casual workers.

The shortage of longshoremen in Halifax was exacerbated by a coincidental shortage of freight handlers, which caused overall productivity in the city to pale in comparison to that in Montreal. The British ministry of war transport oversaw eighty-five percent of all ship movements into and out of Halifax, and in anticipation of a doubling of traffic the coming year, expressed some doubt as to whether Halifax could handle it.

C. D. Howe, never Halifax's friend at the best of times, suggested sending in dockwork-

OPPOSITE
THE RCMP patrol vessel *St. Roch* leaves Halifax for Vancouver via the Northwest Passage, 1944

Cargo waiting to be loaded lines a Halifax dock, 1942

ers from Montreal. Vince MacDonald, the dean of Dalhousie's law school and the arbitrator appointed by the federal minister of labour, had a much more creative solution. He thought the problem stemmed from the system of hiring individual workers on a daily basis at the individual work site, as required. He suggested a central hiring agency and the organization of workers into gangs with permanent bosses or foremen. MacDonald saw stevedoring as a process carried out by the combined activities of several entities, including railways, port officials, stevedoring companies, and longshoremen, all of which had to co-operate and work together in order to achieve better productivity.[12]

As a result of MacDonald's initiative, numerous changes were adopted in the way ships were worked. In March 1943, a central dispatching agency, or manning pool, was established on Hollis Street near the corner of Bishop Street. Workers were to join permanent gangs, and each gang boss was to receive notice as to whether his men were needed on a given day. Gangs were rotated and alternated between day and night shifts. A cargo handler could lose his permit to work on the docks if he did not report for work when called. The new system streamlined the allocation of workers but it did not eliminate worker shortages at peak periods when ships were preparing to sail in convoy. This problem was particularly acute when convoys began using American ports and calling at Halifax on the way by, as high productivity and the quick loading of vessels was essential to keep the convoys on schedule.

In the winter of 1942 to 1943, there were severe labour shortages during peak periods, and the Department of Labour issued strict controls on the supply of waterfront labour. New regulations froze longshoremen in their jobs and sought to bring former longshoremen back from other

Merchant ships berthed in Bedford Basin wait to be loaded or unloaded while freight bound for the Allied armies in Europe arrives in Halifax by rail, circa 1941

occupations. An Order-in-Council provided for a guaranteed weekly wage to ensure an adequate labour force would be available at all times. Stevedoring was given high priority and a longshoremen's reserve pool was established to augment the manning pool. Reserve pool members had to report daily but could also be dispatched to work elsewhere in the city or the Maritime provinces. The purpose of the guaranteed weekly wage was to stabilize the labour supply, provide a means of effective government control, and bring about economic contentment amongst the workers.[13] But this measure was not enough, and further means were necessary to guarantee a sufficient labour pool. In March 1944, the Department of National Defence established the Halifax Port Company, which provided the city with a standing labour supply of three hundred and fifty soldiers. They performed a number of tasks, including ship loading, freight handling, and truck driving. Many also worked at night, when rank-and-file stevedores were still hard to find.

MERCHANT MARINERS

The unsung heroes of the Battle of the Atlantic were the merchant mariners who risked life and limb to make sure their cargoes of provisions and supplies made it through the German gauntlet to feed a hungry Britain. As Rear Admiral Leonard W. Murray, a Canadian naval officer who played an integral part in the Battle of the Atlantic, commented, "The Battle of the Atlantic was not won by any Navy or Air Force. It was won by the courage, fortitude and determination of the British and Allied Merchant Navy."[14] During the war, Canada operated the fourth-largest merchant navy in the world, and most of its ships were built in Canadian shipyards. Much of this merchant fleet was made up of the 176 Park ships, 10,000-ton vessels that were operated by a Crown corporation called Park Steamship Company Limited.[15] The rest of the merchant ships were operated by Canadian National Steamships (CNS) and Imperial Oil. In addition to this, Canadian Pacific had 37 vessels that were registered in Britain but crewed largely by Canadians. More than 25,000 merchant ship voyages were made between Canada and Britain during the Second World War, and 72 Canadian vessels were lost to enemy action. Canada and Newfoundland also lost 1,629 of the more than 12,000 merchant mariners who served on Canadian, American, and British vessels.

ABOVE
Rescued merchant survivors from ss *Milcrest* pose for a wartime photo aboard HMCS *Nanaimo* at Halifax, October 1942.

OPPOSITE TOP
Stevedores loading TNT onto a ship docked in Halifax Harbour, circa early 1940s

OPPOSITE BOTTOM
Cargo handlers loading a truck onto a ship docked in Halifax Harbour, circa early 1940s

MISSIONS TO SEAMEN

The Second World War also brought the establishment of the Halifax chapter of the Missions to Seamen, now called Mission to Seafarers, to provide solace and comfort to visiting seafarers. The mission was a British-based organization originally founded in 1856 as an adjunct to

ABOVE
A wartime poster stressing the importance of secrecy regarding naval and merchant ship sailings

OPPOSITE
V-E Day rioters fill Hollis Street between Blowers and Bishop streets, 1945

the Church of England. It established a presence in Halifax to serve the large influx of British seafarers coming to the city in wartime convoys. Its first home in Halifax was in the Anglican Centre on Barrington Street (now the Khyber Building). Following the war it acquired a building farther south on Barrington Street, where it provided limited overnight accommodation. As the face of shipping changed, the building was sold and in the early 1970s the mission moved to a custom-built mobile home near Pier 24. It has since expanded into a more substantial building in the same location, on land leased from the Halifax Port Corporation.

V-E DAY

The end of the war was a bittersweet time in Halifax. On the one hand, as the *Halifax Herald* headline read, "Halifax treated troops arriving home from WWII to huge celebrations," but on the other, there were the V-E Day riots, which Stephen Kimber has dissected brilliantly in his book *Sailors, Slackers, and Blind Pigs*.[16] The positive role that Halifax played in the war effort was largely overshadowed by the infamous riots, which consumed the city on May 7 and 8, 1945.[17] Prior to V-E Day, civic authorities had warned senior navy personnel that restaurants, cinemas, and liquor stores would be closed to celebrate the hard-earned victory in Europe. Unfortunately, the navy did little to provide troops with food or refreshments or to keep its 18,000 men and women off the streets. The results should have been predictable. Combined with disgruntled locals, who broke into liquor stores and the Alexander Keith's brewery on Lower Water Street, soldiers and sailors participated in what historian R. E. Caldwell has called a "complete breakdown of military good order and discipline."[18] The riots exposed "the seamy side of the war economy, the poor housing," and the strains placed upon the city in performing "its appointed

V-E Day rioters on Salter Street in Halifax, 1945

role," as Jay White argues.[19] By the end of the riot, 564 local businesses had suffered damage, 207 shops had been looted, and 3 rioters were dead. A federal inquiry conducted after the incident placed the blame on the navy for the poor discipline of its personnel. However, in many ways the city was culpable, too, inasmuch as it had not completely adjusted to the overwhelming influx of armed services personnel during the war.

CHAPTER SEVEN

The Winter Port
1946–1970

In the immediate post-war period, the Port of Halifax was back to an uncertain and perhaps frightening reality. As might be expected, within a year of the war's end, cargo volumes had declined more than 40 percent, from 5.7 million tons to 3.3 million tons. Likewise, grain shipments, which were over 50 million bushels in 1944, had declined to 13.2 million bushels in 1946. Vessel arrivals dropped from 3,160 to 2,409, and departures were reduced from 3,219 to 2,414. Not surprisingly, given the numbers of returning military personnel, war brides, and early immigrants, the number of passengers passing through the port peaked in 1946 at 83,721 and quickly declined to 49,030 a year later.[1] With the war over and port activity diminishing drastically, it seemed that Halifax was once again going to be relegated to the status of a winter port.

War brides and children arriving at Pier 21, circa late 1940s

THE WINTER PORT AND IMMIGRATION GATEWAY

Reflecting their reversion to winter port status, both Halifax and Saint John remained in the doldrums throughout the early 1950s. Halifax's total tonnage grew from 3.8 million tons in 1951 to 5.6 million in 1955, while Saint John's increased from 2.3 million to 2.8 million. In stark contrast, cargo totals in Montreal had rebounded from 4.2 million tons in 1943 to almost 11 million in 1947 and 15.8 million by 1955. It seemed, as Bill March and Jay White point out, that having found Halifax useful in wartime, "the national government would once more fail to appreciate the advantages offered by the ice-free, deep-water harbour in peace."[2]

Immigration to Canada resumed in 1947, and the use of Pier 21 as a national gateway peaked in 1951, when 103,682 passengers entered Canada through the facility. Overall post-war immigration to Canada peaked in 1957 with the arrival of 282,000 immigrants, of whom 73,627 passed through Halifax. The tide of immigrants included war brides, most of them from England, Scotland, and Wales, but also some from Holland, France, Belgium, and Italy. They numbered about 48,000 in total and were accompanied by another 22,000 children. The majority passed through the Port of Halifax in 1946 and 1947, and arrived on the Cunarders *Aquitania* and *Franconia* from Liverpool. Besides the war brides, there were also thousands of displaced persons and refugees leaving Europe in the wake of the war, as well as some fleeing from the Communist takeovers of the Baltic states (Estonia, Latvia,

OPPOSITE
Canadian troops returning to Halifax after the Second World War

BELOW
Young boys in the immigration hall at Pier 21, circa late 1940s

The luxury liner SS *Aquitania* berthed at Piers 21 and 22 of Ocean Terminals

and Lithuania), Poland, East Germany, Czechoslovakia, Yugoslavia, and Hungary. It has been estimated that of the 500,000 immigrants who came to Canada in the years immediately after the war, about 100,000 were displaced persons or refugees. Halifax's close proximity to Europe and its year-round port made it the cheapest, quickest, safest, and most logical way to evacuate people from their troubled homelands.

With Europe still in disarray, immigration to Canada continued virtually unabated throughout the 1950s, with Pier 21 averaging 45,000 arrivals annually, about a third of the Canadian total. In the words of Pier 21 historians Trudy Duivenvorden Mitic and J. P. Leblanc, "This was the era of the ocean liner and it was not unusual to stroll the Halifax waterfront and see more than one liner, filled to repletion with new Canadians, gingerly sidle into a berth near Pier 21."[3] However, the facility's use began to decline after transatlantic airplane flight became more prevalent in the late 1950s and early 1960s. Only 20,266 people passed through Pier 21 in 1960, and these numbers proved typical for the rest of the 1960s. By 1970, the number of immigrants entering Canada through Pier 21 had declined even further, and officials decided that there were no longer sufficient numbers of immigrants travelling by sea to support the facility. The doors of the Pier 21 immigration shed were closed on March 28, 1971, just over forty-three years after they were first opened.

HAL BANKS AND THE DECLINE OF THE MERCHANT MARINE

At the end of the war, Canadian National Steamships (CNS) became involved in a labour dispute between the Communist-backed Canadian Seamen's Union (CSU) and the Seafarer's International Union (SIU), which was led by the notorious Hal Banks, a controversial American labour union leader with alleged mob connections. CNS had offered the CSU a new agreement that included a war bonus as part of regular wages, a fifty-two-hour workweek, and a four-hours-on, eight-hours-off watch system, but their wages were to remain at about fifty percent of comparable American wages. As the CNS-owned Lady Boats were now competing with foreign-flagged and foreign-crewed vessels in the West Indies, they could not afford to pay higher wages and still keep their bottom lines in the black. The CSU rejected the deal and went on strike, tying up three CNS-owned vessels, *Canadian Constructor*, *Canadian Cruiser*, and *Lady Rodney*, at Halifax, as well as every other Canadian deep-sea ship under its jurisdiction in any port worldwide. According to Felicity Hanington, "It was the largest, most effective, and costliest strike in the history of Canada's merchant service."[4]

Because of the CSU's Communist influence (a serious liability in the early Cold War context), management at CNS set out to replace the CSU with the SIU, which had agreed to accept the deal rejected by the CSU. In the spring of 1949, tensions mounted. Hal Banks found one hundred seamen to replace the CSU's crewmen, and arranged to have them sent to Halifax, along with another one hundred security personnel from the railway itself. As Hanington tells it, a secret train, "filled with stewards, cooks, firemen and seamen," left Montreal under cover of darkness, and when it arrived in Halifax it pulled into a siding about a mile from where the ships

OPPOSITE
Lady Rodney, shown docked at Ocean Terminals, foreground

were docked. At around 4:00 AM the next day, the SIU seamen were escorted on foot to their assigned ships and, protected by "the CNR Police, and three Union strongmen," brushed aside the pickets and took over the vessels. Hanington describes the scene:

> Emotions ran high on both sides and a battle developed with obscenities and brickbats flying. The CSU was kept at bay by water from high pressure hoses. Amid the deafening noise of the melee a shot was heard. Apparently, it grazed somebody in the crowd. The scene was ugly. Never before had Halifax witnessed such a bitter struggle along her sprawling waterfront.[5]

By the end of the confrontation, the CSU's hold on CN Steamships was broken, and the company's fleet was now crewed by the SIU. However, despite the new agreement with the SIU, labour costs were still rising and were four hundred percent higher in 1951 than they had been in 1939. As well, both passenger transport and cargo shipping were becoming less lucrative for CNS; passenger travel was switching to airplanes, which reduced CN Steamships' customer base, and purpose-built cargo vessels were making inroads on the Lady Boats' cargo. The Lady Boats carried flour southbound and sugar northbound, but neither commodity paid high freight rates and cargo capacity on the vessels was limited. Saguenay Shipping, a CNS rival owned by Alcan Aluminum, was a fierce competitor in the West Indies trade. Saguenay ships carried bauxite, the main ingredient in the production of aluminum, northbound and general cargo southbound in purpose-built cargo vessels. Alcan needed to transport the bulk bauxite from the Caribbean to supply its smelter in Arvida, Quebec, and the general cargo like lumber, groceries, and hardware helped offset the cost of this raw material.

Despite the diminishing market in passenger and cargo transportation, CNS made a small profit in 1956, its first in seven years. But CNS's financial problems were not behind it yet. With the expiry of the SIU's contract in 1957, the union started agitating for a fifty percent raise. CNS countered with an offer of eight percent. The SIU rejected the offer and went on strike in July 1957; the protest saw three ships strikebound in Halifax and another five in Montreal. In response, CNS transferred registry of its vessels to Port of Spain, Trinidad, and hired ninety-five Jamaicans to crew them. Although strikebound, the five vessels were moved with foreign crews from Montreal to Halifax before the onset of winter, where they joined three sister ships, the first time the entire fleet had been together since it was launched in 1929. The Lady Boats continued to run for only a short time longer. Six months after their registry had been transferred, in May 1958, the service was shut down and the "ladies" were put up for sale, as it was no longer financially viable to keep them running. They departed Halifax Harbour in 1958 after twenty-five years of service.[6] In many ways, it was the end of an era, as Haligonians were no longer able to board a ship in their port and sail to the Caribbean.

RETURN TO "NORMALCY"

According to Ray Beck, an engineer who joined the National Harbours Board in 1946 and would go on to become the port's general manager in 1973, "There was lots of construction going on [in the Port of Halifax] in the late 1940s and into the '50s." A $1 million capital works program in Halifax included an extension to the transit shed at Pier 9 and its access road, the construction of Pier A1 at Ocean Terminals, the widening of Marginal Road, the reconstruction of quay walls at Ocean Terminals, improvements to the grain gallery, the purchase of new refrigeration equipment for the cold storage plant, and the construction of a stevedore's canteen.

THE SPECTRE OF THE ST. LAWRENCE SEAWAY

More ominously, the construction of the St. Lawrence Seaway between 1956 and 1959 placed Canada's Atlantic coastal ports in a very precarious position, even though the seaway's impact was not immediately felt. In 1960, Montreal was handling more than twice the cargo tonnage of Halifax (18.2 million tons versus 7.9 million). At that time, Halifax was handling about 3,100 vessels, 20,000 passengers, and 25 million bushels of grain per year. Halifax remained a key regional hub for a vast array of exports, including fish, apples, potatoes, lumber, newsprint, gasoline, and gypsum, as well as wheat, barley, oats, and cereals. Imports included sugar, molasses, crude oil, chemicals, steel, and rubber.

The construction of Pier A1 at Ocean Terminals, 1956

The St. Lawrence Seaway, sometimes referred to as Canada's "fourth seacoast,"[8] reaches from Montreal to the westernmost extremity of Lake Superior, a distance of 2,500 miles (4,000 kilometres). The two partners in its construction, Canada and the United States, had slightly different aspirations for it. The Americans saw it as an inexpensive means for goods manufactured in the industrial heartland to access international markets, while Canada was looking for a cheaper way to ship grain from the Prairies to markets in Europe. Both countries anticipated

OPPOSITE
A soviet communications vessel docked in Halifax Harbour, circa 1960s

benefits to their iron ore and steel industries. In the U.S., the country's railroads and eastern port interests opposed the seaway's construction. In Canada, the Port of Montreal feared some loss of cargo to ocean-going vessels bypassing the port.

After the seaway's construction, its tonnages quickly grew, from about 19 million in 1959 to 45 million in 1965. The largest proportion of cargoes was carried by lakers; ocean-going vessels only represented about one-third of its tonnage. Bulk commodities (grain and iron ore) accounted for the vast majority of the cargo carried. From 1959 to 1965, general cargo increased from 1.7 million tons to 5 million tons. Around the same time, the NHB decided to build a large grain elevator at Port-Cartier, Quebec, to provide storage for grain that would offset iron ore going back up the seaway. Port officials in Halifax were concerned about this decision, as they feared it would cause them to lose potential grain cargoes that could have been railed to Halifax and increase the number of ocean-going vessels entering the seaway to pick up general cargo.

To make matters worse for Canada's Atlantic ports, in the mid-1960s the federal government began icebreaking on the St. Lawrence under the guise of "flood control," but more likely the reason they did so was to support year-round navigation to Montreal. In addition to this problem, the shipping conference system (essentially a system of legalized cartels dating from the nineteenth century) began to charge the same rate to ship to Halifax as they did to Montreal, thus eliminating the advantage afforded by being closer to Europe.[9] Given these developments, one might expect that Halifax cargo volumes would reflect a precipitous decline in fortunes for this period. However, the overall level of growth in the post-war economic boom actually resulted in some cargo *increases* in Halifax at this time, although they were not quite as high as the increases experienced in Montreal and other St. Lawrence ports.

POST-WAR BOOM

From 1960 to 1965, Halifax port tonnage actually grew twenty-five percent, from 7.9 million tons to 9.9 million. The National Harbours Board's local Halifax office was very optimistic about the future. In 1965, it achieved a "record year." By the end of October 1965, cargo was 200,000 tons higher than the previous year, and other increases were also seen in the movement of lumber, vehicles, apples, cement, canned goods, grain products, and manufactured goods.[10]

The cargo-handling boom in Halifax went hand-in-hand with a construction boom. By the end of 1966, the NHB had virtually completed the construction of Shed 33, which was to be used for perishable cargoes in winter. A new marine tower had been built at Pier 26, which would allow for a faster discharge of grain and handling of larger vessels. As well, a new grain conveyor galley had been installed at Pier 28 at a cost of $1.3 million. The port also acquired the area known as Seawall Defence, located between Pier B and the Royal Nova Scotia Yacht Squadron, which was to be the site of a new pier, Pier C. At Pier 9, Industrial Estates Limited announced plans to lease space to Volvo, which intended to relocate its vehicle assembly plant from Dartmouth. As well, a site behind the cold storage facility at Pier 26 was leased to Dover Flour for a milling operation, and the cold storage plant was working at full capacity at this time.

The port was extremely important to the local economy during the early- to mid-1960s. Total jobs were estimated at three thousand in winter and one thousand in summer. The port's various businesses employed twelve hundred longshoremen and nine hundred freight handlers. It was second only to the navy of all major generators of economic activity in Halifax, generating $18.25 million per annum as compared to the navy's $52 million. A report prepared for the

ABOVE
An aerial view of Ocean Terminals, circa 1965

OPPOSITE
Cargo-handlers use a sling to lift a snowmobile, 1949

Atlantic Provinces Transportation Study of 1966 pointed out that the port was very important to the Nova Scotia export trade, as well as those of Newfoundland and PEI, notwithstanding its small natural hinterland and dependence on cost-effective rail access to central Canada and the American Midwest.

THE DOLDRUMS

Unfortunately, the post-war cargo-handling boom did not last long in Halifax. By 1966, ice-breaking and winter navigation were costing Halifax and Saint John about 200,000 tons each of general cargo in winter. As of 1966, Halifax was only getting general cargo in winter when the Commonwealth Preference tariff made New York too expensive. Winter navigation on the St. Lawrence was also problematic. The industrialization of the Quebec north shore in communities like Baie-Comeau, Port-Cartier, and Sept-Îles had led to a change in policy regarding icebreaking. These communities and their industries demanded and received icebreaking as far as Trois-Rivières. Soon, pressure built to extend it as far as Montreal.

In 1957–58, there had been only one shipping line offering winter service to Montreal; by 1966–67, there were six or seven. This was a major threat to Halifax, which expected to drop 750,000 to 1,250,000 tonnes.[11] Overall, despite the level of activity described above, the situation in Halifax was "a sad state of affairs."[12] The situation would get worse before it got better. In 1966, the port experienced further shrinkage in cargo. Newfoundland cargo began moving via North Sydney, Nova Scotia, and Port aux Basques, Newfoundland, and Halifax lost one European and two West Indian shipping lines due to winter navigation and the loss of port parity rates.

There was also still a need for better infrastructure in the Port of Halifax and the province as a whole. Port and provincial leaders appreciated the requirement to develop secondary manufacturing in the region because its economy lagged so far behind the rest of the country's. In order to offset the perceived high cost of rail, which was, according to Ray March of the Halifax Port Commission, "the principle obstacle to the development of secondary industry," an alternative four-lane highway linking Halifax and Truro; Amherst, Maine; and Montreal was proposed by the province and various business groups.[13]

But despite the proposed infrastructure developments to aid Nova Scotia's manufacturing sector, the construction of, and support for, the St. Lawrence Seaway still really stuck in Halifax's craw. The seaway's accumulated deficit at the end of 1965 was already $42 million. Moreover, it was operating with a non-compensatory rate structure, and some MPs wanted to abolish tolls completely. In Ray March's opinion, this was "highly paradoxical" thinking. The seaway was not expected to pay its own way, but there was no compunction about imposing compensatory rates on freight moving by rail to, from, and within the Atlantic region. By this point, some shipping lines, including Far East Line and West Africa Line, had substituted Toronto for Halifax and had saved twenty dollars per ton in doing so.

Clearly, people within the community felt the port was threatened by both the St. Lawrence Seaway and the icebreaking being undertaken on the St. Lawrence. Halifax had lost its winter port status and was struggling to find a raison d'être. According to J. W. E. Mingo of the Halifax Port Commission, Halifax was "dying on the vine."[14] Ray March thought Halifax would lose fifty percent of its general cargo business within two winters if nothing was done. The minister of transport, J. W. Pickersgill, agreed, and told the attendees of the Atlantic Ports Day conference in December 1966 that Halifax "should go after new technology."[15]

THE HALIFAX PORT COMMISSION

Rather than bemoaning their fate, as Haligonians had often done in the past, the Halifax Port Commission responded to the challenges the port was facing in the mid-1960s with bold and effective leadership. The commission had been created by a special act of the legislature in 1952, and had grown out of the Port of Halifax Club, a creature of the Halifax Board of Trade, whose object was "to bring together into an organized body all those interested in the business of the port and the promotion of its fortunes."[16] The original members included R. John Fisher and Harry I. Mathers. The commission, which received an operating grant from the city of Halifax, was intended to (1) promote the development of the Port of Halifax in the best interests of its citizens, and (2) serve as a medium of communication between the National Harbours Board and the City of Halifax.[17]

J. W. E. (Bill) Mingo, chairman of the Halifax-Dartmouth Port Development Commission, presents an inaugural call plaque to an unidentified vessel captain.

In the mid-1960s, the Halifax Port Commission was headed by two visionaries, Ray March, as executive secretary, and J. W. E. Mingo, as chairman. March was born in Glasgow, Scotland, and came to Halifax in 1958 at the age of forty, first working as a reporter with the *Chronicle Herald*, and then with the Halifax Port and Industrial Commission. Mingo was in his mid-forties at the time he joined the commission, and was a well-connected corporate lawyer with Stewart, McKeen, and Covert (now Stewart McKelvey), Halifax's largest law firm.

According to Mingo, some senior civil servants at the time thought the Port of Halifax was "finished" commercially, and that the only new facilities that would be built in the future would be those of a "make work" variety. Nonetheless, the commission urged the NHB to acquire the Seaward Defence and Greenbank properties, which lay between the southern extremity of the board's property and Point Pleasant Park, for the expansion of port facilities. In late 1965, in a "great stroke of fortune," the Department of National Defence expressed an interest in exchanging its Seaward Defence site for piers 2 and 3 and paying the NHB an additional $4 million for the property.[18] The NHB accepted the deal, and secured the Greenbank property shortly thereafter. By early 1966, the board had a twenty-three-acre site suitable for the construction of a container terminal, although the idea of using it for this purpose only developed gradually.

THE CONTAINER REVOLUTION

In the meantime, a new form of cargo-handling and shipping technology based on the use of containers was being introduced in a number of locales. The invention of container shipping is usually credited to an American trucker named Malcolm McLean, who first introduced it on a service from New York to Puerto Rico, and Matson Line, which operated from the U.S. mainland to Hawaii. However, the concept of containerization may have actually been invented in Canada in 1953, when the ferry *William Carson*, built for Canadian National Railways, was outfitted to carry containers of 3' × 2'6" on CN's service between North Sydney and Port aux Basques. Five additional prototypes of 10' × 6'4" × 8'4" were built the same year. As well, the Port of Vancouver claims that the Canadian company White Pass & Yukon introduced the first purpose-built container ship on its route from North Vancouver to Skagway, BC, in November 1955, carrying commercial 8' × 8' × 7' containers, each with a capacity of five tonnes.[19]

Like all revolutionary ideas, containerization had its doubters and skeptics, and as a result, the "revolution" did not take hold until the mid-1960s, even though it was considered by some to be "the most important development in international transport service since the change-

Arthur Krueger, the first purpose-built container ship to visit Halifax, 1969

Greenbank, shown here in 1953, was one of two South End properties acquired for the purpose of building a container terminal.

over from sail to steam."[20] The primary reason for the delay was the huge capital costs that ports and shipping companies had to incur to enter this new business. But the increased efficiency in cargo-handling, lower freight charges, and rise in trade flows that were direct results of the container revolution eventually won over even the staunchest skeptics of container shipping, and containerization was embraced as the harbinger of a new era of commercial shipping.

THE KAUFFELD REPORT

In 1966, the Halifax Port Commission hired John Kneiling, an eccentric New York engineer who worked for industry consultant Theodore J. Kauffeld, to examine the feasibility of developing a container gateway to North America at Halifax. Kneiling's report described a very exciting future for Halifax as a gateway to North America. According to Kneiling, the key to the port's future "was its 70' [21 m] deep harbour (compared to New York's 45' [45 m] or Montreal's 35' [11 m]), which would make Halifax the only port in North America capable of handling superships of 200,000 tons and up." Kneiling envisioned "a 'supership' shuttle between Rotterdam and Halifax, with 70 mph turbotrains [at the time of Kneiling's report, CN had just introduced its passenger TurboTrain between Montreal and Toronto] hauling seven-mile-long strings of container cars deep into the U.S. and Canadian west, at the same time knocking 25 percent off shipping costs."[21]

Kneiling also emphasized that Halifax was 550 nautical miles (1,000 kilometres) closer to Europe than any port in North America, and was only 25 miles (40 kilometres) from the Great Circle Route on the North Atlantic. With a deepwater draft of 45 feet (14 metres) alongside to handle the predicted giant container ships of the future, Kneiling contended that Halifax

Harbour was a natural centre for container traffic, as well as warehousing, assembly, and transport to inland markets in Canada and the U.S. In addition, Kneiling argued that Caribbean feeder services would enhance Halifax's status as a transshipment base. Kneiling promised that when he was finished, "they would only use the Seaway for canoe races."[22]

Kneiling's report was not quite ready when the country was swept up in Trudeaumania in the late 1960s. However, when asked what the federal government could do for Halifax, certain influential Liberals suggested the construction of a container terminal. The result was Pierre Trudeau's promise, issued from the steps of Halifax City Hall during the 1968 election, to build a new container terminal in Halifax. The promise caught the NHB bureaucrats in Ottawa by surprise, as they had anticipated that all containers would be handled at the newly built private container facility in Montreal. But Trudeau told them to "make it happen" in Halifax. In December 1968, the Department of Transport in Ottawa made the official announcement that a container terminal would be built in Halifax, only six months after Trudeau's election as prime minister.

THE DEVELOPMENT OF HALTERM

Thus ensued the construction of the Halterm container facility at Pier C, to the south of Ocean Terminals and adjacent to Point Pleasant Park. The site chosen was the most expedient one available at the time, and had actually been acquired by the NHB in 1967. The facility was to be developed in three or four phases over several years and would comprise three berths of 700 to 800 feet (215 to 245 metres) in length, with water depths alongside of 35 to 50 feet (10 to 15 metres). Initially, there would be 20 acres of backup land with another twenty-five available later.[23]

Not surprisingly, the site earned its share of criticism for its encroachment on Point Pleasant Park and the South End neighbourhood, especially from the press. Bill Mingo remembers taking Graham Dennis, owner of the *Chronicle Herald*, out for lunch, to try to get the press to back off. They did, and the terminal went ahead with construction at a cost of $14.5 million. The NHB filled in parts of the harbour to create the land on which the container terminal would sit, and the terminal operator equipped it with container-handling equipment. When it was completed, the facility covered 56 acres in total, including a circular rail track with capacity for 272 railcar spaces and 100 electric plugs for refrigerated containers. As well, two container gantry cranes were designed, erected, and installed by the NHB and leased to Halterm on a buy-back basis, with the first crane going into service in November 1970.

An early container vessel docked at Pier B of the Halterm facility, with construction of the Pier C container terminal underway in the background, 1970

One of the problems to be worked out once the terminal was completed in 1969 was who would operate it. By this time, the NHB was supportive of the project and it wanted to run the terminal. CN had also expressed interest in running the facility. However, the terminal's first would-be customer, Clarke Traffic Services (through the newly formed Dart Containerline consortium), vetoed these proposals. It fell to Bill Mingo to decide who would

ABOVE AND OPPOSITE
Aerial views of the Halterm Container Terminal construction site, 1967

run the facility. His solution to the problem was to give control of the terminal to Halterm Ltd., a consortium made up of Halicon (Halifax International Containers Limited—itself an 80:20 joint venture between the provincial and municipal governments), Clarke, and CN. The role of Halicon in this project was to market container transportation via Halifax and, if necessary, charter space at volume discounts not available to individual shipping lines on CN unit trains. Halterm Ltd. negotiated a ten-year lease on the facility with the NHB, and Clarke agreed to manage the terminal on behalf of the consortium. In October 1969, F. H. "Joe" Howard, an erudite railway man "with great personality and interest in transportation" from London, Ontario, was hired as president of Halicon, and Brian Doherty, a hard-nosed stevedoring executive from Quebec City, became manager of the terminal itself.[24]

In July 1969, Dart Containerline began operating from Pier B of the Halterm facility with three small chartered vessels of just over 200 TEUs each, running a weekly service connecting Antwerp, Amsterdam, Rotterdam, Southampton, Halifax, and New York. This service paved the way for them to acquire three purpose-built, fully cellular vessels of 1,556 TEU capacity, which commenced service from Halifax in the fall of 1970. In combining calls at both Canadian and U.S. ports with greatly increased vessel size and capacity, the new Dart service took full advantage of all of Halifax's positive attributes. As historian Peter Hunter explains, "Dart had aimed for and settled on big ships, a Northern Atlantic shore port, liner trains, and trucks inland, sufficient containers of the right types to accommodate the traffic envisaged... and a port that could readily serve both Canadian and U.S. trades."[25]

Halifax was the first port in North America to do direct ship-to-rail container trans-

fer. Stanley Clarke, the owner of Clarke Traffic Services and one of the partners in Dart Containerline and Halterm Ltd., supported the idea of ship-to-rail container transfer, proclaiming, "This is the way it's going to be done." The inauguration of Dart Containerline's service to Halifax was a quantum leap forward, and it thrust CN into the role of a major container mover, especially since the transfer of containers straight from ships onto trains was a practice that most U.S. ports did not exploit until well into the 1980s. As well, CN's ship-to-rail transfers revolutionized the way shipping rates were calculated; shipping lines could now quote through rates that included the haulage to the port in Europe, terminal costs in Europe, time at sea, terminal costs at Halifax, and the rail haul from Halifax.[26]

Port labourers' opinions were more complicated when it came to containerization, as stevedores were concerned with job losses through mechanization and unitization. A container terminal could load and unload as much cargo in twenty-four hours as a conventional vessel would take in two weeks. Containerization was also a way to cut down on pilferage, which had become endemic in places like New York and Montreal.[27] Port labour had always been a part-time occupation that attracted farmers and fishermen who would have otherwise been unemployed in winter. But the containerization revolution was a chance to professionalize the industry and bring some stability to the lives of stevedores and others involved in the port industry. As "port historian" Herbie Westlake of the International Longshoremen's Association recalls, when containerization was introduced, about ninety percent of the port's cargo was break bulk and the port employed around five hundred men, mostly part-time. Containerization was a challenge for labourers to accept because initially it would mean that only fifty men would be employed. However, these fifty men would be employed full-time. As well, containerization would finally make Halifax a year-round port, which would mean that stevedores would have work during all seasons, not just winter. Westlake and the members of the association understood that the port had to become a gateway for Canada, as ninety percent of the cargo would be moving inland to Montreal and Toronto. While it may have taken some time for the members of the International Longshoremen's Association to come around to the idea of container-shipping, they eventually hailed it as "a godsend."[28]

THE REVOLUTION TAKES ROOT

While Dart Containerline was already using the new container terminal, Halifax was also seeking to attract other shipping lines to call at Halterm. One of the main lines it courted successfully was Atlantic Container Line (ACL). Reflecting the enormous capital costs involved in containerization, ACL was formed in 1966 and was a consortium of traditional European shipping companies, including the venerable Cunard Steamship Company of the U.K.; Swedish America Line, Trans-Atlantic Steamship Company, and Wallenius Line, all of Sweden; International Transport of Holland; and Compagnie Générale Maritime of France. The consortium's first vessel to dock at Halterm was *Atlantic Cinderella*, a unique $13-million, 696-foot (212-metre), roll-on, roll-off container ship, which the Halifax *Mail Star* described as a "silver slipper."[29]

As historian Peter Hunter points out, "Scandinavian influences ran deep at ACL," as the company was the first major carrier to incorporate both lo-lo (lift-on, lift-off) and ro-ro (roll-on, roll-off) technology into the same vessel. (Scandinavian shipping companies, such as Wallenius Line, had pioneered the development of roll-on, roll-off vessels to carry trailers

Dart containers being unloaded at Pier A1, 1969

The container ship *Jorg Kruger* and Dart containers at Pier A1, 1969

across the Baltic, and are still pioneering in this sector with huge new vessels catering to the "short sea" market.)³⁰ ACL also introduced combination vessels that carried three types of cargo: 20- and 40-foot containers, which were stacked in "cells" by massive container gantry cranes; containers and other cargo on mafis (low-profile steel-wheeled trailers that are loaded with cargo that is otherwise difficult and cumbersome to handle), which were rolled on; and wheeled vehicles such as autos and heavy equipment, which were driven on board. ACL's vessels proved to be ideally suited to the needs of Volvo's Halifax auto manufacturing facility, which had been operational since the early 1960s. Complete, knocked down (CKD) units from the Volvo plant were loaded on mafis, while finished vehicles were driven on board for export to the U.S.

Within a very short period of time, Halterm attracted several other carriers, notably the German companies Columbus Line, which operated from Halifax to Australia and New Zealand, and Hapag-Lloyd, which served the North Atlantic trade in competition with Dart and ACL. As well, in 1972, the Israeli line Zim Israel Navigation Ltd. augmented its Mediterranean–Great Lakes service by establishing Zim Container Service, operating on a "pendulum" schedule between Hong Kong and Haifa, Israel, via the Panama Canal. This new service provided Canadian and Atlantic region shippers with outlets to the Mediterranean, the Far East, and the Caribbean. According to Robert Kaye, a marketing assistant at the port commission, staff at the commission were so busy in the early 1970s that they were unable

Dart containers leaving Halifax through the rail cut, 1969

to meet with a delegation from ACT/PACE Line, which served Australia and New Zealand, so the company took its business to Saint John instead.

Halifax had thrust itself into a new league of "container ports." Montreal had beaten Halifax to the container market by a year, but Halifax had been the first port in the country to build a common-user container facility (a facility that was available for use by a variety of clients as opposed to a private terminal for one shipping line). The expensive new container technology left out many other regional ports in Canada, with only Halifax, Saint John, Quebec City, Montreal, and Vancouver being able to muster the financial resources to construct the necessary terminal infrastructure. In 1970, Halifax handled 20,800 TEUs and was one of 90 ports worldwide with container facilities. Total port tonnage topped 11.5 million tonnes that year, a 10 percent increase over the previous year and a new record. General, or break-bulk, cargo dropped 10 percent, but containers more than made up for the difference. By 1972, Halifax handled almost 86,000 TEUs and was ranked 32nd of the 105 container ports worldwide in terms of cargo handling. Containerization now also brought many unforeseen benefits to local industry, increasing the port's hinterland and giving longshoremen the opportunity to earn a regular (and higher-paying) living.

THE CHANGING FACE OF HALIFAX

The face of Halifax changed dramatically in the twenty-five years after the Second World War. The Macdonald Bridge was built in 1955, opening up the city of Dartmouth to both residential and industrial development. The community of Africville was razed in the 1960s and eventually made way for the McKay Bridge. Scotia Square replaced the slums just north of city hall with several high rises. Perhaps because the old district of finger piers along Lower Water Street had fallen into disrepair, a harbour freeway was planned to run from the city's first spaghetti interchange at Cogswell Street, along the harbourfront, up Point Pleasant Drive, and across the Northwest Arm to Spryfield. Luckily, it was stopped dead in its tracks by a group of citizens who considered heritage to be as important, if not more important, than progress. In the South End, perhaps because the port and its fortunes are part of each Haligonian's DNA, the story was different, and the construction of the Halterm facility had proceeded with little protest. The impact of the facility on Halifax was not unlike similar impacts elsewhere, according to historian Frank Broeze:

A view of the Halifax waterfront taken from George's Island in the 1950s. If planners had gotten their way in the 1970s, a freeway would have been built along the harbourfront. Instead, a restoration project has revitalized the area.

> To be part of the new container world, ports need to undergo a complete metamorphosis. Container terminals must have huge slabs of open, but well founded, space to park and arrange containers for shipment; appropriate equipment to move containers across the terminal; specialized container cranes; and ideally, on-the-spot connections with rail, road and/or water transport facilities. [...] With the exponential growth of container shipping the ports of the world had to undergo dramatic physical transformations, in which the traffic that previously had been handled by large numbers of individual

THE WINTER PORT, 1946–1970   163

wharves, finger piers and docks were now centralized in a handful of huge terminals. More often than not such space could not be made available in existing conventional port areas.[31]

Fortunately, Halifax was able to provide the required space and amenities needed for the container facility. The result was a terminal that is still the envy of the shipping world, with a deep, ice-free, natural harbour and almost immediate access to North Atlantic shipping lanes.

CHAPTER EIGHT

The Container Age
1971–1998

The 1970s saw the containerization of the major trade lanes of the world, including the North Atlantic, trans-Pacific, and Europe–Far East. The 1980s were marked by the remarkable rise of Asian shipping lines such as Evergreen Marine, as well as three main trends: larger vessels capable of carrying up to 3,000 TEUs, round-the-world services, and the establishment of large load-centre ports (ports that could serve more than their immediate markets). These developments heavily favoured Nova Scotia's only container port, Halifax, especially over its once archrival, Saint John. By the 1990s, containerization had fully established its supremacy in the shipping world, and traditional break-bulk cargoes had all but disappeared.

HINTERLANDS AND CARGO

With the advent of containerization, Halifax truly became Canada's Atlantic gateway. Some examples of Nova Scotia and Atlantic region cargoes carried by container during the late twentieth century include:

Commodity	Destination(s)
blueberries	Japan and Germany
apples	U.K.
seafood	Europe, Caribbean, Far East
peat moss	Far East
newsprint	U.S., Europe, Far East
french fries	Europe, Far East, Australia
lumber	Europe, Middle East, Far East
ambulances	Middle East
tires	Europe, Far East, U.S.
flour	Iceland

By the 1970s, Halifax had four main hinterlands: the Atlantic provinces, central Canada, the U.S. Midwest, and New England. It also served both Newfoundland and New England via feeder vessels. Ironically, very little port-related manufacturing or distribution activity actually took place in Halifax, as eighty percent of the cargo handled in the port originated in or was destined to its hinterland. Nevertheless, it was estimated that one out of seven jobs and over $1 billion in economic activity was generated by port activity during this time.

Prior to containerization, small shippers of apples or fish in the Annapolis Valley or the Digby area had to pool their resources and charter a reefer (i.e. refrigerated) vessel of about 3,000 tons. With the advent of containerization, these same suppliers could ship their product one container at a time, in lots of ten to twenty tons. Nova Scotia's fruit shippers, including apple and blueberry producers, were amongst the first to adapt to the new reefer technology in the early days of container shipping. In fact, they pooled their resources, and with government support, purchased a fleet of refrigerated containers for use by ACL and Hapag-Lloyd. Gradually, seafood producers also adopted this new means of transportation, as it vastly cut down on the need for storage and allowed product to be shipped fresh. By 1990, shippers such as Comeau Seafoods in Saulnierville had completely switched from reefer vessels to reefer containers.

Most of the impact of containerization in the province was actually felt outside Halifax, in places like Granton (rubber inbound, tires outbound), Bridgewater (tires), Waterville (tires), Abercrombie (wood pulp), Port Hawkesbury (newsprint and super-calendar paper), Mahone Bay (plastics), Lunenburg (fish), Meteghan (fish), Kentville (fruit and vegetables), Wolfville (apples), Oxford (blueberries), Yarmouth (ambulances), Bridgetown (elastic), and Digby (scallops). Containers have made it much easier for Nova Scotia shippers to access every corner of the globe.

By the early 1990s, the traditional method of break-bulk shipping had been totally usurped by the container's efficiency, economy, and ease of handling. More than ninety-five percent of the world's general cargo shipping was handled in containers. Every major, and even minor, trade was now containerized, offering low-cost, frequent service to shippers of all sizes. This is one of the most positive aspects of containerization, which in many ways presaged the advent of globalization and the rise

The stern of a Hapag-Lloyd vessel laden with containers, 2005

ABOVE
A Halterm gantry crane lowering a container onto a truck, 2005

OPPOSITE
Gantry cranes handling containers at the Halterm facility, 2005

of the so-called Asian "Tigers." In 1970, the total value of the world's merchandise trade was $300 billion. In 1995, global trade had reached $4.7 trillion, thanks in large part to the container. Virtually every nook and cranny in the world was now accessible to the container, allowing large and small shippers alike to access markets worldwide.[1]

THE GATEWAY STUDY

One of the ironies of containerization in Halifax was that relatively few companies in the city were dependent upon the facilities that handled containers. In 1976, it was estimated that a mere forty companies located within Metro Halifax used the container terminal.[2] By 2000, that total was much higher, but most local industries still did not use the container facilities in the port. The city's industrial parks tended to be distribution or warehouse facilities as opposed to manufacturing plants. Most of the direct employment from containerization actually went to longshoremen, truckers, shipping agents, freight forwarders, customs clearance officers, harbour pilots, and terminal and port administrators, not factory workers. The city's focus on transshipment as opposed to manufacturing, as well as its location and natural virtues, made it an ideal candidate to act as a gateway to the rest of Canada.

The gateway concept envisioned Halifax hosting dozens of companies that would import products that could be processed or manipulated in the city and then shipped to central Canada, the U.S., or Europe. The concept was studied quite extensively in the 1970s, most notably in a

seminal study called "Feasibility of Developing a Transportation Gateway for North America at Halifax" by the firm Arthur D. Little Inc.[3] It was an old idea dating back to at least the days of Joseph Howe. The idea was viewed in glowing terms by the federal Department of Regional Economic Expansion (DREE), whose 1975 Subsidiary Agreement with the Province of Nova Scotia states:

> Because of its favourable location on the north Atlantic trading routes, Halifax-Dartmouth may have a unique viable opportunity to create from 1,000–35,000 jobs as a transshipment and warehousing centre for goods and products imported into North America from Europe, Africa and western Asia, and vice versa. […] The scheme would call for construction of giant warehouses to house the goods and related control systems and hardware. The Halifax-Dartmouth Metropolitan area could become a centre of expertise in container traffic management.[4]

For various reasons, the gateway initiative was not particularly successful, but it did identify several strengths and weaknesses in Halifax's competitive position vis-à-vis other ports.[5] Halifax's advantages included its proximity to Europe; ample space for expansion in the port; the availability of government incentives; excess capacity in terminal facilities; underutilized but experienced labour; and good intermodal connections. Balanced against this were the following disadvantages: a complex administrative structure for the Port of Halifax; a lack of scheduled air cargo flights from Halifax; the lack of marine feeder service between Halifax and U.S. East Coast ports; Halifax's cost disadvantage over Baltimore and New York for goods destined for the U.S. Midwest; the port's inferior rail connections to the U.S. Midwest; low labour productivity (based on 1972 data); and relatively high cost.

Along with these disadvantages, G. B. Norcliffe, author of a study on industrial development in Halifax, comments that there was "little evidence of existing shippers wanting to open containers at a warehouse operation near Halifax for sorting, storing and re-shipping. On the contrary, the aim was to avoid double-handling by loading boxes onto rail-cars and moving them to central Canada unopened and with minimal delay."[6] As a result, companies like Canadian Tire would ship imports from the Far East through Halifax for warehousing and storage in Toronto, then ship them back to their stores in Atlantic Canada. Clearly, Halifax *was* a gateway, but not of the type envisioned by John Kneiling and others.

MORE CHANGES AT THE PORT

Halifax built on its early success with containerization until the early 1980s, handling over 200,000 TEUs annually and ranking in the top five North American East Coast ports and in the top thirty worldwide. In 1981, however, Dart Containerline stunned port officials with its announcement that it would combine its service with Manchester Liners and CP Ships at Montreal, and take over one-third of the port's business with it. A short time later, another company, Trans Freight Lines (TFL), also announced its departure from Halifax.

The same year that Dart announced its departure, the government of Nova Scotia appealed the creation of the St. Lawrence Coordinated Service, a new entity owned by Dart, Manchester Liners, and CP Ships, to the Canadian Transportation Commission (CTC).[7] It complained that CN's eighteen percent holding in CAST, a unique container and bulk carrier that operated between Montreal and Antwerp, constituted a conflict with its Halifax-based

business, which had included Dart. The agreement between CN and CAST had been to use CP Rail to transport goods whenever possible, which, in turn, meant that goods would need to be shipped through Montreal instead of Halifax. Testimony by shipping analyst Michael L. Sclar highlighted the emergence of two vertically integrated transportation groups in Canada. Locals feared that this development could have far-reaching impacts on shippers in the Maritimes, especially if services to world markets were lost. If Maritime shippers were faced with trucking cargo all the way inland to Montreal to be shipped overseas from there, they would lose their locational advantage. Sclar argued on behalf of the Province of Nova Scotia that this was not in the national interest. Nonetheless, the CTC eventually ruled that the new St. Lawrence service could proceed.

The provincial government then appointed a group called the Grice Committee to investigate the role of the port and the various agencies involved in port promotion. It recommended the disbanding of Halicon and the takeover of the Halifax Port Commission by the province, together with an infusion of funds to hire more staff and undertake more travel, research, and advertising. John Grice, a stevedoring contractor who specialized in the offshore oil and gas sector, and who had at one time been the port commission's executive director, became chairman of the commission. The executive director of the commission, Gary Blaikie, stayed on for a few more years before being replaced by Victor Bayne, who had been director of marketing with Halicon before becoming the agent for Polish Ocean Line.

ABOVE
An aerial view of the Fairview Cove berth extension, 1985

OPPOSITE
Construction of the first phase of Fairview Cove Container Terminal, 1980

Ships berthed at Fairview Cove, 1986

There were several changes happening at the National Harbours Board during this era, as well. In 1982, the NHB was renamed the Canada Ports Corporation, and on June 1, 1984, the Halifax Port Corporation (HPC) was established as one of its subsidiaries. Ray Beck remained on as port manager for three more years, retiring in 1984, but came back later as the HPC's chairman. David Bellefontaine, a certified management accountant who had joined the NHB on December 1, 1968, became president and CEO of the HPC in 1984. His executive team included Robert Kaye, director of marketing; Dennis Creamer, director of finance and administration; Dick Pentland, director of engineering; and Captain Claude Ball, harbour master and director of operations. The HPC was quasi-independent; its board consisted of local representatives appointed by Ottawa, and it still needed federal approval for such items as land exchanges, some contracts, and long-term leases. However, the board was given some latitude on easement agreements and short-term leases.

Another change to take place at the Port of Halifax in 1981 was the opening of a second container terminal at Fairview Cove, which was operated by Ceres Incorporated of Chicago. Despite the setbacks of losing Dart and TFL, developments in the container industry still appeared to be working in Halifax's favour.

PROSPERITY REIGNS

Aggressive marketing by both the Halifax Port Corporation and the Port Development Commission began to pay off in the 1980s. For a while, it seemed as if there was a new ship arriving every week. During the middle part of the decade, the port attracted Polish Ocean Line, Sea-Land, ABC Containerline, Nordana Line, Djakarta Lloyd, Atlantraffik Express Service, Compagnie Maritime d'Affretment (CMA), National Shipping Company of Saudi Arabia, Jebsen Line, Scan Carriers, ACT/PACE, Ocean Star Container Line, Shipping Company of Trinidad and Tobago (SCOTT), Orient Overseas Container Line (OOCL)/Neptune Orient Line (NOL)/Kawasaki Kisen Kaisha ("K" Line), and Maersk Line. However, some of these services were longer-lived than others, as the marketplace was constantly in flux.

In 1986, the Halterm terminal managed to snag one of the new round-the-world services operated by Tricon, a consortium of OOCL, of Hong Kong, NOL, of Singapore, and "K" Line, of Japan. The Tricon service operated on an eastbound round-the-world route utilizing nine 3,000-TEU vessels and calling at twenty-four ports on a sixty-three-day cycle. The vessels called at Halifax to pick up Canadian cargo and to top off, as their loaded draft of forty-two feet (thirteen metres) was too deep for New York. They usually stayed in port for thirty-six hours, during which time they would load and unload up to fifteen hundred containers, or fifteen to twenty thousand tonnes of cargo. (This amount of cargo would have taken ten days to handle using conventional cargo-handling methods.) When they set sail from Halifax, the vessels did not see a port again until they reached Singapore twenty-one days later.

By the late 1980s, Halifax had attracted over twenty-five shipping lines, which were moving almost 450,000 TEUs through the port annually. In 1987, after much study and several attempts to find a potential operator, a new short sea feeder service between Halifax and Boston commenced, predicated on the schedule of the Tricon service mother ship calls. A year later, the Danish Maersk Line, at the time one of the largest container lines in the world, began a new North Atlantic import and Far East export service via Halifax. By the end of the decade, Halifax boasted "more services to more world ports than any other port in Canada." It seemed that it was on the threshold of load centre status, more than doubling its container volume and approaching to within 50,000 TEUs of Montreal by 1989. Although it had not yet made any significant inroads in the U.S. Midwest, Halifax served markets in Atlantic Canada, Quebec, Ontario, and New England.

RIVALRIES

The container industry initially bypassed secondary ports, as the capital requirements were simply too onerous for smaller ports to contemplate. Hence, only two container ports emerged in Atlantic Canada in the early years of containerization, at Halifax and Saint John. The only other ports with container facilities in Canada at this time were Quebec City, Montreal, Vancouver, and Fraser River. Quebec City was the original container terminal for CP Ships, but it ceased to be a player in containerization in the early 1980s when CP moved its operations to Montreal, citing the latter's closer proximity to markets. Saint John and Halifax were rivals until the late 1980s, when Halifax won out because its location on the Great Circle Route required no deviation off the main shipping lanes, whereas a call at Saint John required that a vessel transit around the tip of Nova Scotia and up the Bay of Fundy.[8] By 2000, Saint John had just one container service, owned by the Irving Group, but the port had made a speciality of handling forest products and other niche cargoes.

The situation on the U.S. East Coast was perhaps more dramatic. The initial round of containerization resulted in there being only one container port in New England, at Boston. In 1999, Boston handled slightly fewer than 90,000 TEUs, compared with 462,000 TEUs at Halifax. Boston was easily served by truck or barge from New York or by smaller feeder vessel from Halifax, and it lacked efficient intermodal connections to any kind of hinterland beyond New England. The age of the container had introduced Montreal, New York, and Norfolk, Virginia, as Halifax's greatest competitors for port traffic, while its old rivals of Boston, Quebec City, and Saint John aggressively pursued other business opportunities, such as bulk cargo and forest products.

LABOUR IN THE CONTAINERIZED PORT

From a labour perspective, while containerization meant that it took fewer people less time to move more cargo, thereby reducing the number of cargo handlers needed, it also benefited stevedores because it turned the Port of Halifax into a year-round operation, thus eliminating the need for them to find employment in the off-season. Whereas in days gone by longshoremen had to supplement their labour by fishing and lumbering, in the years since the container revolution it has been possible to earn a substantial, full-time living as a longshoreman. By the end of the 1990s, longshoremen were among the highest paid industrial workers in the world.

In the last decades of the twentieth century, the largest longshoremen's union in Halifax was Local 269 of the International Longshoremen's Association, which was founded in 1908. At one time, it had as many as 1,800 members, but they basically only worked from December to April when the St. Lawrence River was closed to navigation and Halifax was a winter port. But after containerization, the number of union members dropped considerably. In 2000, the longshoremen's union had only 264 members, while the other port workers' unions were even smaller; the checkers' union had 76 members, the maintenance workers' and gearmen's union had 55 members, and the watchmen's union had 2 members.

After the container revolution, the longshoremen's union and their management group, Halifax Employer's Association, established predetermined qualifications for joining Local 269. Prospective members had to pass aptitude and machinery tests, as well as undergo alcohol and drug testing. Most longshoremen agreed that containerization had been a positive development for the Port of Halifax. It had professionalized their occupation, making it more lucrative, and brought Halifax from a winter port to a year-round operation.

On board the ships themselves, changes to employment were no less sweeping. Modern container ships introduced in the 1980s had as few as twelve to fourteen crew members, many of them highly trained. In most cases, sailors from container ships never came ashore because their jobs did not end once the vessel docked. The vessels only stayed in Halifax for eight to ten hours, and there was much to do while the ship was in port. Occasionally, crew members would need medical attention, groceries, or personal effects, but their main onshore activity tended to be a visit to the Missions to Seamen to call home, borrow a book, or chat. Due to the quick turnaround of vessels, ports generally had little character for sailors spending time ashore.

The crews of modern-day container ships tend to be multinational. Officers are often of the nationality of the shipping line, but crew members tend to be from the developing world.

Typically, crews work six months on, six months off, or less commonly, three months on, three months off. While conditions on board many bulk and tramp ships had often been abominable, those on board a typical container ship can be quite luxurious. ACL's large G3 container ro-ro vessels, for instance, are equipped with a small indoor pool, a squash court, a gymnasium, and a pub.

THE ECONOMIC IMPACT OF THE CONTAINERIZED PORT

In 1979, the Port of Halifax published its first "Economic Impact" study to help it secure funding for the container terminal at Fairview Cove. At that time, it was estimated that the total direct, indirect, and induced benefits of the Port of Halifax amounted to $824 million.[9] The total employment impact was almost eight thousand jobs, or one out of ten jobs in Metro Halifax. Although break-bulk cargo had the highest impact on the city per tonne, container cargo was projected to have the greatest future potential impact. The study recommended that containerization be promoted by finding local Atlantic-region cargoes that could be containerized and by developing port services such as marine insurance, ship repair, and consolidation services.

The 1979 study was updated in 1991 by Gardner Pinfold Consulting Economists, though their methodology of calculating the port's impact on the local economy had changed somewhat from the earlier study.[10] According to the new study, the total income impact of port activities was now $282.2 million, and the total employment impact was 8,712 jobs, or 1 in 19 in Metro Halifax, or $1 of every $15 in household income. The total direct impact of vessel disbursements was $111 million, of which $62 million was accounted for by container vessels, reflecting how well-ensconced containerization had become even since the earlier study. General cargo (break bulk) and vehicle-carrying vessels had greater per-tonne impacts, but much smaller volumes than containers. Total direct expenditures in the 1991 study amounted to $355 million, including vessel disbursements, crew expenditures, cruise passenger expenditures, surface transportation, and general services.

The 1991 study was in turn updated in 1997. This time, the report claimed total direct expenditures of $3 million to $5 million, GDP income impact of $520 million, and employment of 7,750.[11] Containers and container ro-ro vessels accounted for by far the largest economic impact, at $369 million and 6,200 jobs. Next highest were pure vehicle ro-ro vessels of the kind that called at Autoport, at $56 million and 300 jobs. The latter activity also had the highest impact per tonne of cargo handled, followed by container ro-ro vessels, general cargo, and then container vessels.

RESTRUCTURING

Halifax's newfound prosperity was short-lived, as structural changes within the industry reduced the port's container tonnage back to its 1980 levels by 1992. New trends saw mergers, slot charters (sharing space on a competitor's vessel), and realignments among various hitherto competitors. As well, in the early 1990s, many lines, most notably the Tricon service operated by OOCL/NOL/"K" Line, backed off their round-the-world strategies in favour of adding additional "strings" in particular trades, such as the trans-Pacific.(A "string" refers to a fleet of vessels required to serve a particular trade route.) The Tricon service needed nine vessels on a sixty-three-day rotation to provide a weekly service from the Far East to the U.S. East Coast. Those same nine vessels were redeployed in two separate strings of four and five vessels to provide two separate services from the Far East to Los Angeles–Long Beach and from the Far East to Seattle. The new strategy meant that the same vessels were able to provide a higher frequency of service, thus giving the shipping line better productivity from its capital assets. Some lines had as many as six different services, serving North Asia–North Pacific, South East Asia–Southern California, and so on.

The last decade of the twentieth century also saw the development of huge hubs in Hong Kong and Singapore to serve the burgeoning Chinese and Southeast Asian markets. Each of these ports handled over 16 million TEUs, nearly twice the volume of Los Angeles–Long Beach, the largest port complex in North America.

The Port of Halifax adjusted to these changes by attracting so-called Suez express services directly from Southeast Asia and serving the Midwest via CN's new St. Clair Tunnel. But its biggest market, the North Atlantic, was impacted by the re-emergence of Montreal, which now handled twice the container volume as Halifax. With the full support of CP Railways, Montreal had become the most cost-competitive route to the Midwest, and a convenient way to avoid the prying eyes of U.S. shipping legislators. Along with Canada-Maritime and CAST, owned by CP Ships, by the late 1990s Montreal had added a separate North Atlantic service operated by Maersk, Sea-Land, and P&O Nedlloyd.

Within a generation, Halifax slipped from thirty-third to eighty-sixth in world container port rankings. Despite increases in container tonnage, it continued to lose market share to its largest Canadian competitors, Montreal and Vancouver. Montreal's container traffic grew to 993,486 TEUs in 1999. Vancouver's performance was even more impressive; through innova-

OPPOSITE
An aerial view of the Autoport facility, 1981

tive and aggressive marketing (and some good luck) it leap-frogged over Montreal and surged 27 percent to 1,070,171 TEUs in 1999, and it would top 1.5 million TEUs by 2003. By comparison, Halifax's volumes were very uneven. In 1997 it handled 459,176 TEUs, but fell 7.3 percent to 425,435 TEUs in 1998 before increasing 8 percent in 1999 to 462,766 TEUs. Thus, in effect, Halifax's traffic had increased less than 1 percent over three years, and had barely squeaked past totals that were attained in the late 1980s.

Fifteen years previously, changes in the container industry had heavily favoured Halifax. In the early 1990s, structural change within the industry had a deleterious effect on Halifax, and it lost both volume and significant market share to rivals such as Montreal and Norfolk. A similar fate befell Baltimore, which slipped from a 13 percent share of 540,770 TEUs in 1989 to 486,861 TEUs, or a 9 percent share, in 1998. Likewise, New York, which increased its volume from 1.9 million TEUs to 2.4 million TEUs, still saw its share fall from 47 percent to 44 percent in the same period. The winners in this battle were Montreal (which increased from 522,451 TEUs, or a 12 percent share, in 1989 to 932,701 TEUs, or a 17 percent share, in 1998) and Norfolk (which grew from 685,371 TEUs, or a 16 percent share, in 1989 to 1.2 million TEUs, or a 23 percent share, in 1998).

A DIVERSE CARGO BASE

Other cargoes besides containers were also handled at Halifax and they often provided substantial economic spinoffs, helping to boost the port economy when times were tough in the container industry. One such cargo is automobiles, which were handled at the Autoport facility after it was opened in 1970. Autoport, located in Eastern Passage, is an import/

A Volkswagen Bus being loaded onto a railway flatcar at Pier A1, 1959. Dockside handling of automobiles improved dramatically with the opening of the new Autoport facility in 1970.

export automotive terminal, originally predicated on moving European imports such as Volkswagens westbound to central Canada and sending domestic vehicles eastbound for distribution in Atlantic Canada. Both moves tend to balance each other out, thus reducing transportation costs for manufacturers and consumers.

The facility itself did not change much from the time it was originally built to the late 1990s, except that a new office building and service depot was added. In 1999, it comprised approximately 100 acres, with capacity for about 12,000 cars. There were two wharves, of 660 feet (201 metres) and 404 feet (123 metres), capable of accommodating the largest car carriers afloat, such as those operated by Wallenius Whilhelmsen and VAG Transport, which could carry up to 7,000 vehicles. A CN rail spur and five loading tracks were also part of the complex.

At the turn of the twenty-first century, Autoport handled approximately 100,000 cars per annum. Customers included Mercedes Benz, BMW, Audi, Volkswagen, Saab, Volvo, Jaguar, Land Rover, Honda, Mazda, Toyota, Nissan, GM, and Ford. European imports were typically offloaded directly from the vessels, while Japanese imports were brought in by rail from Vancouver. Occasionally, a vessel would come all the way around from Japan to Halifax via the Panama Canal, but this was a rarity. Some domestic vehicles were exported to Europe, but most vehicles handled at Autoport were destined for the Atlantic region. Vehicles destined for

Newfoundland were loaded directly from Autoport onto the vessel *Sanderling*, which was operated by Oceanex.

However, the most significant break-bulk commodity handled at the Port of Halifax was not automobiles, it was forest products. A new specialized terminal for forest products was constructed at piers 26 and 27 in 1997, and it was operated by Logistec Inc., which also operated a much larger facility at Saint John called Forterm. The facility in Halifax included a 65,000-square-foot (6,000 square-metre) shed that was specifically engineered for handling and storing forest products. It had vertical stacking capability of 20 to 25 feet (6 to 7.5 metres) and other features needed for handling wood pulp. Regular break-bulk liner services such as Hoegh Lines, Wallenius Whilhelmsen, and National Shipping Company of Saudi Arabia used the facility.

Halifax also handled about four million tons of gypsum per annum during the late twentieth century. It was mined by National Gypsum, a U.S. company, near Lantz, Hants County, and shipped in dry bulk ships to markets along the U.S. East Coast. Tonnages depended upon the state of the U.S. office- and home-construction business. It is interesting to note that gypsum was exported in raw form and imported back into Canada in at least 128 different commodities, ranging from drywall to mascara. Numerous studies have been done to examine the potential of manufacturing drywall, in which gypsum is a key component, in Nova Scotia, but both the fragility of the product and the cost of shipping have always stood in the way.

In the days prior to containerization when Halifax functioned as one of Canada's winter ports, grain was also an important import and export commodity. But changes in Canada's grain markets and the elimination of transportation subsidies in the late 1980s changed the whole

A CN train beside the Halifax Grain Elevator, 1964. At the time this photo was taken, approximately 100 railcars of grain were being unloaded per day, with 320 cars waiting to be dumped. Volumes at the facility dropped greatly at the end of the twentieth century when Pacific ports began handling the majority of Canadian grain.

structure of grain shipping in Canada. Since 1987, over half of Canada's wheat exports have moved via Pacific coast ports. About ninety-five percent of East Coast grain exports are now handled in Quebec at Montreal, Sorel, Trois-Rivières, Quebec City, Baie-Comeau, and Port-Cartier. Typically, East Coast grain exports are shipped in lakers to a St. Lawrence River port, where they are stored in large grain elevators prior to being loaded into ocean-going bulk vessels. Whatever grain is left over is handled at Churchill and Halifax.

The Halifax Grain Elevator, leased to private operators since 1985, continued to play an important role in providing feed grain for farmers in Nova Scotia throughout the end of the twentieth century. The elevator handled grain imports by both rail and water, but only an insignificant amount still arrived by rail, as the rail lines now competed with all-water shipments. Whereas the grain elevator was once very busy in the winter, most of its imports now arrived, ironically, when the St. Lawrence Seaway was *open*. It handled four main products at this time: export wheat, domestic wheat destined for Dover Flour next door, domestic feed grains for farmers in the Maritimes, and exports of wood pellets. The elevator handled about 300,000 tons of product per annum and upwards of twenty vessels. Overall, it was operating at about twenty percent of capacity throughout the 1980s and 90s, although there were many times during the year when it was full.

Although all of these commodities contributed to the Port of Halifax's viability, the vast majority of the port's non-container cargo tonnage in this period was represented by petroleum products shipped to and from one of the two active oil refineries in the Maritimes. Crude oil was handled inbound from Venezuela and other offshore suppliers, while refined oil was loaded out for distribution in domestic markets in the Atlantic region. Some heavy fuel oil was also imported directly to the Nova Scotia Power generating station at Tuft's Cove in Dartmouth. When the Sable Gas Lateral Pipeline was extended to that location in 2000, it was expected to have an effect on crude oil tonnage. Petroleum tonnage also varied according to

FOLLOWING PAGE TOP
The Sedco 704 drilling rig in Basin 1, Ocean Terminals, 1984

FOLLOWING PAGE BOTTOM
An aerial view of offshore supply vessels docked at Richmond Terminals, 1983

BELOW
The oil tanker *Esso Copenhagen* in Halifax Harbour, 1981

market conditions, the severity of winter, the amount of summer air conditioning, and other factors. In 2000, the port handled 3.3 million tonnes of crude oil; this grew to 3.8 million in 2001, but it was back at 3.3 million in 2002, suggesting that the pipeline had only had limited effect on crude tonnages. Refined oil peaked at 2.2 million tonnes in 2000, and had fallen to 1.2 million by 2002.

Since the 1970s, the Port of Halifax has also played host to a variety of offshore drilling programs and their attendant supply base activity. The first supply base was located at Woodside, on the Dartmouth side of Halifax Harbour, where Mobil Oil ensconced itself in the early 1970s. The Mobil facility in Woodside included a small dock and open area and extensive pipe storage of fifteen to twenty acres across Pleasant Street in the Woodside Industrial Park, which had a wharf of 330 to 360 feet (100 to 200 metres), with backup of less than five acres.

In 1982, Shell established a supply base at Pier 9. Husky–Bow Valley followed only a few years later. Its facility was made up of four berths, ranging in length from 456 feet to 787 feet (139 metres to 240 metres), and total open areas of just under ten acres. As well, PanCanadian's supply base for its Cohasset-Panuke field was located at Pier 9 of Richmond Terminal until 1998. As of March 2000, the Port of Halifax has also been host to the Sable consortium's (SOIE) supply base.

ABOVE
OOCL *Thailand*, a post-Panamax vessel with a 5,770-TEU capacity, visits the Ceres container terminal in Halifax.

PREVIOUS PAGE
OOCL *Chicago*, the stern of which is featured in this 2006 picture taken at Halifax, was considered a behemoth among container vessels until the development of a new monster-sized class of post-Panamax vessels in recent years.

THE POST-PANAMAX ERA

The end of the twentieth century saw the arrival of ever-larger ships in Halifax. In the mid-1980s the so-called G3 vessel of 3,000 TEUs, 40,000 tons, and about 1,000 feet (300 metres) in length was considered to be very large. Indeed, the 3,014-TEU vessels of the OOCL/NOL/"K" Line consortium, which commenced calling at Halifax in May 1986, were among the largest vessels of their kind in service at the time. Container vessels broke the so-called Panamax barrier of 106 feet (32.32 metres) in width and 4,500 TEUs in capacity in the late 1980s, with the first order by American President Lines. Since then, vessels have become bigger and bigger, and their appetite for cargo has grown unabated as they move into new markets and new commodities. Vessels topped out at around 5,000 TEUs in the early 90s until the Danish-owned Maersk Line introduced the *Regina Maersk* in 1995. This 6,000-TEU monster called at Halifax in July 1998 to underscore the Maersk Sealand superport bid process, which had short-listed Halifax, New York, and Baltimore as potential sites for a new East Coast hub. New York eventually won the bid, but Maersk Sealand committed to continue visiting Halifax as a port of call and stated that the Port of Halifax would factor into its plans for future growth. Even though Halifax may not have won the Maersk bid, its participation in the competition, and its subsequent receipt of a spot on the short list of contenders, helped secure its reputation as a port capable of handling post-Panamax vessels and put it on the map in the post-Panamax shipping world, broadening its scope for opportunity in the future.

CHAPTER NINE

Canada's Atlantic Gateway
1999–2008

A number of significant developments took place at the Port of Halifax during the final years of the twentieth century. On July 1, 1999, Pier 21 opened as a museum paying tribute to over a million immigrants, refugees, troops, and war brides who passed through the facility. A cruise pavilion was also opened nearby in Shed 21 South, built at a cost of $1 million. In 2000, Halterm and the Halifax Port Authority came to an agreement on the renewal of the South End container terminal lease, and in July of that year, in a bold move pointing towards the future, Halterm took delivery of two post-Panamax cranes at a cost of $23 million.

The 1990s also witnessed changes of great significance in the structure of Canada's port system. Following several years of discussion and negotiation, Canada's major ports urged the passage of new legislation that removed some of the barriers in their path. The Canada Marine Act of 1998 granted local port authority status to Canada's major ports and

Halifax's downtown core has undergone a stunning metamorphosis in recent decades, incorporating eighteenth century heritage features such as the Citadel fortifications and the historic properties along its waterfront with twenty-first-century high-rises and port facilities.

instituted a policy of commercialization. As the new millennium approached, the Port of Halifax seemed to be completing a full circle since Confederation, with administrative control having moved from local decision-making under the Halifax Harbour Commission, to central control under National Harbours Board, to more autonomy under the Canada Ports Corporation, and finally once more to local decision-making under the newly formed Halifax Port Authority.

HALIFAX PORT AUTHORITY

The Halifax Port Authority (HPA) received its letters patent on March 1, 1999. The era was ushered in under the leadership of David Bellefontaine, as president and CEO, and a board of directors, the members of which were appointed under a new system of shared governance. Although the majority of board members were still appointed federally, the new legislation provided for direct appointments by the provincial government and the Halifax Regional Municipality, as well as a process of consultation with port users for other nominations. The first HPA board included the internationally renowned lawyer and business executive Sir Graham Day, Alan Abraham Jr., J. Gregor Fraser, Gerald McConnell, Joseph Randell, Elaine Gordon, and Merv Russell as chair. The port's senior management included David Bellefontaine as CEO, Patricia McDermott in marketing, and Dennis Creamer in finance and administration.

Shortly after the foundation of the HPA, with the port's fortunes in local hands, the provincial and municipal governments disbanded the Port Development Commission. The HPA's annual report for 1999 stated that its biggest challenge would be operating competitively within the "environment of greatly reduced fiscal involvement by the federal government."[1] This comment demonstrated one of the new challenges imposed by the Canada Marine Act—ports were no longer able to access any federal loans or funding, nor could they mortgage the properties over which

TOP
Exterior of the Pier 21 shed

LEFT
An immigration officer at the Pier 21 Immigration Museum

The Port Stakeholders, with the port administration building in the background

they were given administrative control.

After David Bellefontaine retired in 2001, the Halifax Port Authority changed leadership. Karen Oldfield, a St. Mary's- and Dalhousie-educated lawyer and former senior civil servant, became president and CEO of the HPA in 2002. One of the first strategic initiatives under Oldfield's leadership was the development of Smart Port, a forum to involve the wider community in discussing and resolving issues of port competitiveness and productivity, identifying value-added opportunities, and addressing security issues in the post-9/11 world. Smart Port undertook a number of studies, including a container growth strategy, a rail optimization study, and a Greater Halifax distribution study, amongst others. Another recent initiative under the new leadership was the formation of the Halifax Gateway Council, which has brought together both private- and public-sector community stakeholders committed to aggressively developing the transportation infrastructure in the region and seizing new opportunities afforded by the surge in business from Asia. Proving the port's benefit to the city, province, and region has never been an issue—the port is obviously one of the pillars of the local economy, generating about fifteen thousand (direct, indirect, and induced) jobs and $1.5 billion in economic output—but these strategic initiatives readily illustrate the HPA's determination and the commitment of its partners in the wider community to finally realize the port's full potential.[2]

THE "CHINA EFFECT" AND SUEZ STRATEGY

The big story in the early years of the twenty-first century has been the so-called "China Effect," which has seen as much as thirty percent of the world's industrial capacity shift to China.[3] As of

The OOCL container vessel *New York* leaving Halifax Harbour

2007, the top five container ports in the world were located in the Far East. Singapore was the largest, followed by Shanghai, Hong Kong, and Shenzhen, China. In Europe, Rotterdam was the largest port, followed by Hamburg, then Antwerp. In North America, the port complex at Los Angeles–Long Beach was by far the largest. Many ports worldwide, especially those handling significant amounts of cargo from the Far East, have seen double-digit growth, fuelled largely by the spectacular growth of China. The Port of Shanghai has risen from comparative obscurity to become the second-busiest container terminal in the world, with ambitions to become the biggest.

OPPOSITE
Dredging the Fairview Cove container terminal

New York was by far the largest port on the East Coast of North America in 2007. In the North Atlantic, it was followed by Norfolk and Montreal. Halifax was at the top of the next tier, ahead of Baltimore, Philadelphia, and Boston. Its old rival, Saint John, handled half the volume it did in the 1980s. (In the southeast, Savannah, Charleston, and Miami handled more containers than Halifax, but those ports do not compete with Halifax.)

Due to its small local market, Halifax is a so-called "discretionary port" (as opposed to a "must call" port), but it serves many markets beyond Atlantic Canada, including Quebec, Ontario, the U.S. Midwest, and New England. Most vessels calling at Halifax do so on their way to or from New York. However, Halifax has a unique advantage vis-à-vis New York, as many vessels use Halifax to top off or lighten up after leaving or before arriving at the harbour in New York, the draft of which is not deep enough to accommodate many post-Panamax ships when they are fully loaded.

As it has from the beginning, in the twenty-first century Halifax continues to face challenges relating to the small local market and the perennial issue of providing cost-effective and efficient access to inland markets. And the competition is not standing still, either. The ports of New York, Norfolk, and Montreal are all in the process of expanding. In the meantime, Halifax has quietly embarked on its own capital investment program, and is currently in the middle of a five-year, $100 million capital investment plan. This program includes deepening the container piers down to fifty-five feet (seventeen metres), making them the deepest berths on the East Coast of North America. Under the leadership of the HPA, the Port of Halifax is facing its competitive future with a new attitude of confidence, summarized in the words of its CEO: "Bring it on!"[4]

THE CRUISE INDUSTRY

Halifax has a long tradition in the passenger shipping business, dating back to the age of sail, and, of course, the Cunard Steamship Line. The cruise industry as we know it today began in the early 1970s when commercial air travel began to supplant traditional passenger shipping. Even though "cruises" had taken place in the 1920s and 30s from New York, the first new-generation "cruise ship" called at Halifax in 1980, when Royal Viking Line brought one of its beautiful vessels to town.

Until recently, Halifax attracted most of its cruise passengers as an integral part of the Canada–New England fall foliage markets, drawing between fifty and sixty ships per year. In 1999, Carnival Cruise Line introduced its 3,600-passenger *Carnival Triumph* ship on three- and four-day cruises between New York, Halifax, and Saint John, and changed the whole complexion of the industry in Atlantic Canada. Since 1997, passenger throughput has almost quadrupled at Halifax, and the city is now an established port of call on three routes: Transatlantic, Canada–New England, and Coastal East.

In September 2004, Halifax hosted Cunard's new *Queen Mary 2*, then the largest passenger ship in the world, built in France at a cost of $800 million. This spectacular liner, which specializes in transatlantic voyaging in the tradition of Cunard's first venture, is five times longer than Cunard's first steamer, *Britannia*, at 1,132 feet (345 metres), with a beam of 135 feet (41

Pipers and the town crier welcome a cruise ship to Halifax

ABOVE AND PREVIOUS PAGE
Cunard Line's *Queen Mary 2* navigates through Halifax Harbour, 2004

metres) and gross tonnage of 151,400 tonnes. It carries 2,620 passengers and 1,253 crew members and cruises at 30 knots. Appropriately, two years after *Queen Mary 2* visited Halifax, a statue of Sir Samuel Cunard was unveiled outside the port authority administration building on the occasion of another visit by the ship.

In 2002, the port and other partners retained consultants to study the potential of attracting home port operations for cruise lines. Although it is not expected that the port will become a jumping-off point for large mega-ships, it may be possible to attract home port or turnaround operations for small- to medium-sized vessels. However, at the time of their study, the consultants identified a principal missing ingredient in this plan: sufficient airlift capacity. Nonetheless, the study predicted that Halifax could attract a large number of new passengers, depending upon how aggressive it is in pursuing the business and whether it is able to attract transatlantic, luxury, and specialty cruise home port operations. Rather than constructing new cruise ship facilities to meet the increasing demands, the consultants' strategy was to spread cruise operations along the seawall and as far south as Pier 30–31. In 2006, the HPA also opened the Cunard Centre at Pier 23, intended to accommodate both home port operations and large events. That same year, three small vessels did turnarounds at Halifax, with more expected in the future.

HALIFAX SEAPORT

A very exciting development currently underway in the Port of Halifax is the redevelopment of the seawall, which promises to bring a dramatic change in the city landscape and the way the port physically relates to the city. Anticipated for completion by 2010, the concept of the project is to redevelop and rejuvenate old, underutilized facilities complementary to the port's cruise business, making them a focal point both for the citizens of Halifax and visiting tourists. The overall design of the redevelopment was led by Toronto's Eberhard Zeidler Partnership, which worked in conjunction with the local architecture firm Lydon Lynch. Zeidler is famous for having designed Toronto's Eaton Centre and Ontario Place. Lydon Lynch has designed most of the new buildings along Halifax's waterfront, including Bishop's Landing and the original Sheraton waterfront hotel (now the Halifax Marriott Harbourfront Hotel). Port man-

Samuel Cunard's great-grandsons at the unveiling of the Cunard statue, 2006

ABOVE
A rendering of the planned Shed 22 building at the Halifax Seaport

TOP
A rendering of the planned Shed 22 building as seen from the water

agement and the project team looked at similar developments in Vancouver, Seattle, and Toronto when developing the plans for the revitalization of the area. The development, to be known as the Halifax Seaport, will be a mixed-use group of facilities centring on the cruise industry, arts, and culture. Artists' renderings suggest a festival atmosphere in a district resembling Vancouver's Granville Island and Baltimore's Harborplace.

One component of the Halifax Seaport that has already opened is the NSCAD University Port Campus, which was designed by award-winning Halifax architect Brian MacKay-Lyons. Another component, which should be opening in 2010, is a new building for the Halifax Farmers' Market. In 2007, the Halifax Farmers' Market announced an ambitious plan to relocate from its current site at the old Keith's Brewery building to the Halifax Seaport development. The market plans to build a new environmentally friendly building at Pier 20. Designed by Lydon Lynch architects, it will be powered by wind turbines, heated by solar power, and cooled by ocean breezes, and it will have a green roof where farmers can grow produce.

CANADA'S ATLANTIC GATEWAY

Since before Confederation, Halifax has seen itself as a gateway port. The monthly magazine

Conceptual sketches of the
Halifax Seaport

CANADA'S ATLANTIC GATEWAY, 1999–2008   203

RIGHT
A 1933 HHC ad touting Halifax as "Canada's Atlantic Gateway"

OPPOSITE
Post-Panamax cranes unloading containers from OOCL *Chicago*

204   CANADA'S ATLANTIC GATEWAY

CANADA'S ATLANTIC GATEWAY, 1999–2008   205

of the Halifax Harbour Commission, published through the early 1930s was, in fact, called *The Open Gateway*. Halifax also once advertised itself as the "Emerging Giant," on account of its ability to accommodate the largest vessels afloat while offering minimal diversion from the Great Circle Route. It has prospered on the inability of New York to accommodate ships drawing more than forty-two feet (thirteen metres), necessitating lightening or topping off at a deeper port. It has also provided a comparatively fast and efficient alternative for cargo destined to and from the American Midwest, especially since access to this large and important market was vastly improved with the expansion of CN's Sarnia Tunnel in 1995. This allowed double-stacked railcars to pass under the St. Clair River and theoretically travel non-stop from Halifax to Chicago. The Port of Halifax has long touted its natural attributes of location on the Great Circle Route, deep water, minimal tides, and ice-free waters. With a weak Canadian dollar throughout most of the 1990s and into the 2000s, it was also cost competitive. Given the investments that continue to be made in competitor ports, the challenge for Halifax is to retain these advantages, generate new opportunities, and capitalize on its long-promised potential. The port finally began to see its natural attributes being recognized when, in early 2006, OOCL introduced the first regular calls of post-Panamax

ABOVE
Breaking ground at the new FastFrate transload centre

OPPOSITE
Super-post-Panamax cranes unloading containers from OOCL *San Francisco*

ABOVE
An oil rig in Halifax Harbour

TOP AND OPPOSITE
Aerial views of the Halterm container facility, now owned by Macquarie Infrastructure Partners

vessels to Halifax with the arrival of the 5,714-TEU OOCL *Chicago* as part of the Grand Alliance AEX Service.

Between 2005 and 2006, two more developments that predict a bright future took place in the Port of Halifax. The first was the agreement signed by the Canadian Retail Shippers Association to ship four thousand containers per annum through Halifax, to be transloaded at a facility owned by Armour Transportation Group. The cargo will either be trucked to inland markets or moved by rail in Armour-branded containers. Since five container-loads of cargo can fit into three highway trailers, the end result is that truck movements are balanced off and containers remain in Halifax where they are needed to load exports. By de-stuffing the containers in Halifax, the scheme also offers the opportunity to distribute the cargo directly to the retailer. The second development took place in early 2006, when Consolidated FastFrate announced that it would build a 150,000-square-foot (14,000-square-metre) transload centre in the Burnside Industrial Park. This facility adds another piece to the puzzle, enabling the port to attract additional Chinese and Indian subcontinent traffic and better serve local markets. A recent study commissioned by the HPA and conducted by Drewry Shipping Consultants confirmed that the Panama Canal and many U.S. West Coast ports were approaching capacity, creating potential opportunities for Suez-based services that would avoid West Coast congestion. Before the new facility was built, containers from Southeast Asia would flow through the Port of Halifax to a distribution centre in Toronto, be broken into shipments on a store-wide basis, and then be trucked back to the Maritimes. Containers would often be empty on their way back to Halifax, as would the highway trailers on their way back to Toronto. The result of the new facility is better asset utilization and access to empty

Aerial view of the Cerescorp terminal at Fairview Cove

containers where they are needed.

As far as the future is concerned, Halifax still has a lot of untapped potential. With a little imagination, it is not hard to envision the Port of Halifax handling over 1.5 million TEUs. At some point in the future, both container terminals in Halifax will be expanded further. Certainly, that must be what Macquarie Infrastructure Partners were thinking when they purchased the Halterm container facility for over $170 million at the beginning of 2007. Also in 2007, Cerescorp Company/NYK expanded its capacity at the Fairview Cove facility by purchasing two super-post-Panamax cranes and building a new state-of-the-art truck gate complex, which goes along with new rail infrastructure recently installed by the port authority.

There are several ideas for future projects at the Port of Halifax that could also help it achieve economic success. A distripark, or logistics park, has been announced for the north end of the Burnside Industrial Park, which could attract new carriers and more shippers to use the port with the establishment of further transload and distribution centres. Short sea shipping might connect Halifax to numerous destinations along the eastern seaboard and possibly into the Great Lakes and St. Lawrence. With EnCana Corporation's Deep Panuke and ExxonMobil's Sable II projects underway, Haligonians should also continue to see oil rigs and supply boats plying the harbour waters. Perhaps one day there will also be a cruise ferry connecting the traditional trading partners of Halifax and Boston, similar to those operating in Scandinavia. It is also not beyond the realm of possibility that locals will see fast ferries in the harbour, carrying passengers between downtown Halifax, Bedford, Purcell's Cove, Shannon Park, and Eastern Passage.

As Karen Oldfield says, Halifax should continue to buy shoes "one size too big." Whatever the future holds, one thing is certain: the port will continue to be the linchpin of the local economy and Halifax's most important and enduring asset.

An aerial view of Halifax Harbour

APPENDIX

Halifax Port Administration

PORT ADMINISTRATION FROM 1867 TO DATE

Organizational Name	Years	Governing Federal Legislation
Halifax Port Authority (HPA)	1999 to date	Canada Marine Act
Halifax Port Corporation (HPC)	1984–1999	Canada Ports Corporation Act
Ports Canada—Port of Halifax	1983–1984	Canada Ports Corporation Act
National Harbours Board (NHB)	1936–1983	National Harbours Board Act
Halifax Harbour Commission (HHC)	1928–1936	Halifax Harbour Commissioners Act
Department of Marine & Fisheries	1867–1928	British North America Act

PORT CHAIRS AND DIRECTORS FROM 1928 TO DATE

"Port Authority" Chairs	Years	Directors
Mark MacDonald, Chair Halifax Port Authority	2007 to date	Trevor Johnson (2007–present), David Henderson (2007–present), Tom McInnis (2008–present), Anne Galbraith (2008–present)
Ian Oulton, Chair Halifax Port Authority	2005–2007	Mark MacDonald (2005–present), D. Geoffrey Machum (2006–present), Linda Moreash (2006–present), William Richardson (2005–2008), Judy Steele (2004–2007)
Alan R. Abraham, Jr., Chair Halifax Port Authority	2002–2005	Gerald Blom (2002–2008), Graham Downey (2003–2006), Barbara Kane (2003–2006), J. Gregor Fraser (1999–2005), Elaine Gordon (1999–2004)
Mervyn C. Russell, Chair Halifax Port Authority	March 1999–2002	Merv Russell (1999–2002), Alan R. Abraham, Jr. (1999–2005), Gerald McConnell (1999–2003), Joseph Randell (1999–2003), Sir Graham Day (1999–2000), Ian Oulton (2001–2007)
Mervyn C. Russell, Chair Halifax Port Corporation	April 1994–March 1999	Merv Russell (1994–1999), David Jones (1994–1999), Linda Brennan (1995–1999), Edward Kirby (1995–1997), Robert Wilson (1995–1999), Howard McNutt (1997–1999)
Lois A. Glibbery, Acting Chair Halifax Port Corporation	January–April, 1994	George Briand (1992–1995), Graham Thomas (1992–1996)
Donald A. Parker, Chairman Halifax Port Corporation	1988–1993	Lois Glibbery (1988–1995), Ernest Coates (1988–1995), Harald Norve (1988–1994)
Raymond V. Beck, Chairman Halifax Port Corporation	1985–1988	Donald Parker (1985–1994), Paul Murphy (1985–1994), Michael Proude (1986–1992), Florence Irwin (1986–1992), Raymond Beck (1984–1988)
Raymond W. Ferguson, Chairman Halifax Port Corporation	March–October, 1984	Gerald Simmons (1984–1988), Hugh MacLeod (1984–1986), John E. Lloyd (1984–1985), Brenda Shannon (1984–1986), Peter Green (1984–1985), Rae Austin (1984–1985), Raymond Ferguson (1984)

PORT CHAIRS AND DIRECTORS FROM 1928 TO DATE, CONTINUED

"Port Authority" Chairs	Years	Directors
Gerald E. Simmons, Chair Halifax Port Authority (Local Advisory Council under NHB)	1971–1983	(National Harbours Board, Ottawa)
E. Hawken, President Halifax Harbour Commissioners	October 1935–1936	A. E. Dubuc, B. J. Roberts
J. L. Hetherington, President Halifax Harbour Commissioners	December 1933– October 1935	F. P. Merchant, O. P. Goucher
E. C. Phinney, President Halifax Harbour Commissioners	September 1930– November 1933	J. L. Hetherington, F. P. Merchant
Peter R. Jack, President Halifax Harbour Commissioners	January 1928– September 1930	Charles W. Ackhurst, John Murphy

PORT MANAGERS FROM 1935 TO DATE

Port Managers	Years
Karen Oldfield	December 2001 to date
David F. Bellefontaine	December 1984–July 2001
Raymond V. Beck	1973–June 1984
John E. Lloyd	March 1971–March 1973
J. R. Mitchell	1953–1968
R. W. Hendry, M.B.E.	1936–1952
F. C. Cornell	1935

Notes

Foreword

1. Joan M. Payzant, *Halifax—Cornerstone of Canada*, (California: Windsor Publications, 1985), 15.
2. David C. McCullough, address at Wesleyan University, 3 June 1984, quoted in James B. Simpson, *Simpson's Contemporary Quotations* (Boston: Houghton Mifflin, 1988).

Introduction

1. *Halifax, Canada's Atlantic Port: Always Open to All Shipping*, Port Brochure, (Stellarton, NS: Nova Scotia Museum of Industry, 1930).
2. Ibid.

Chapter 1

1. Thomas H. Raddall, *Warden of the North* (Toronto: McClelland and Stewart, 1971), 3.
2. Ibid., 5.
3. Ibid., 11; David Sutherland, Judith Fingard, and Janet Guildford, *Halifax: The First 250 Years* (Halifax: Formac Publishing, 1999), 9; Margaret Conrad and James K. Hillier, *Atlantic Canada: A Region in the Making* (Don Mills: Oxford University Press, 2001), 80; Etienne Taillemite, "La Rochefoucauld de Roye, Jean-Baptiste-Louis-Frederic de, Marquis de Roucy, Duc d'Anville," *Dictionary of Canadian Biography*, Vol. III. Sutherland says there were 61 vessels, Raddall says 71, and Conrad says 54. Sutherland says the vessels carried 11,000 sailors and soldiers while Taillemite says 7,006.
4. Thomas B. Akins, *History of Halifax City* (Dartmouth: Brook House Press, 2002), 8. Originally printed as *Collections of Nova Scotia Historical Society*, Vol. VIII, 1895.
5. Donald F. Chard, "Joshua Mauger," *DCB*, Vol. IV.
6. Akins, *History of Halifax City*, 136.
7. See Faye Margaret Kert, *Prize and Prejudice: Privateering and Naval Prize in Atlantic Canada in the War of 1812*, Research in Maritime History, No. 11, 1997.
8. Brian Cuthbertson, *Voices of Business: A History of Commerce in Halifax, 1850–2000* (Halifax:

Metropolitan Halifax Chamber of Commerce, 2000), 9. Cited from *Acadian Recorder*, 14 May 1814.
9. Ibid.
10. Ibid.; and Julian Gwyn, *Excessive Expectations: Maritime Commerce & the Economic Development of Nova Scotia, 1740–1870* (Montreal and Kingston: McGill-Queen's University Press, 1998), 48

Chapter 2
1. David A. Sutherland, "The Merchants of Halifax," PhD thesis (Toronto: University of Toronto, 1975), 153.
2. Eric W. Sager, *Maritime Capital: The Shipping Industry in Atlantic Canada, 1820–1914*, (Montreal and Kingston: McGill-Queen's University Press, 1990). See also W.T. Easterbrook and Hugh G.J. Aitken, *Canadian Economic History* (Toronto: Macmillan of Canada, 1956), 237–238.
3. Eric W. Sager, "The Shipping Fleet of Halifax, 1820–1903," unpublished paper presented to the Atlantic Canada Studies Conference, Fredericton, 1978.
4. Ibid.
5. James D. Frost, *Merchant Princes: Halifax's First Family of Finance, Ships and Steel* (Toronto: James Lorimer and Company, 2003), 50.
6. Ibid., 51.
7. NSARM, Shubenacadie Canal Papers, MG 24, Vols. 37–41.
8. Halifax *Morning Chronicle*, 5 September 1857; *Novascotian*, 12 October 1857.
9. John Hawkins, *Captains, Mansions, and Millionaires: The Remarkable Story of Maitland, Nova Scotia* (Hantsport, NS: Lancelot Press, 1996).
10. Eric W. Sager, "'Buying Ships and Selling Dear': Merchant Shipowners and the Decline of the Shipping Industry in Atlantic Canada," in Peter Baskerville, ed., *Canadian Papers in Business History*, Vol. I (Victoria: Public History Group, University of Victoria, 1989), 59–74.
11. Phyllis R. Blakely, "Samuel Cunard," *DCB*, Vol. IX.
12. Ibid.
13. Ibid.
14. "Ships and Seafarers of Atlantic Canada," Maritime History Archive, Memorial University of Newfoundland, 1998. CD-ROM. Calculations by the author.
15. See Stephen Fox, *Transatlantic: Samuel Cunard, Isambard Brunel, and the Great Atlantic Steamships* (New York: HarperCollins, 2003).
16. Marilyn Gurney-Smith, *The King's Yard: An Illustrated History of the Halifax Dockyard* (Halifax: Nimbus Publishing, 1985), 10.
17. Ibid., 11.
18. Judith Fingard, *The Dark Side of Life in Victorian Halifax* (Halifax: Pottersfield Press, 1989), 17.
19. Judith Fingard, *Jack in Port: Sailortowns of Eastern Canada* (Toronto: University of Toronto Press, 1982), 126.
20. Blakely, "Samuel Cunard."
21. David Nason, *Railways of New Brunswick* (Fredericton: New Ireland Press, 1993), 13; A. A. den Otter, *The Philosophy of Railways: The Transcontinental Railway Idea in British North America* (Toronto: University of Toronto Press, 1997), 73.
22. Joseph Howe to Earl Grey, 29 August 1850, in Joseph Andrew Chisholm, *Speeches and Letters of Joseph Howe*, Vol. II (Halifax: Chronicle Publishing, 1909), 97.
23. Ibid., 116.
24. Ibid., 107.
25. See Allan Jeffrey Wright, "The Method of Friendly Approach: Portland, Maine, as Canada's Winter Port." MA thesis (Fredericton: University of New Brunswick, 1976).
26. Greg Marquis, *In Armageddon's Shadow: The Civil War and Canada's Maritime Provinces* (Montreal and Kingston: McGill-Queen's University Press, 1998), 37.
27. Ibid., 45
28. David A. Sutherland, "Benjamin Wier," *DCB*, Vol. IX.

29. Marquis, *In Armageddon's Shadow*, 211–240.
30. Ibid., 232.
31. Ibid.
32. Province of Nova Scotia, *Submission of its Claims with Respect to Maritime Disabilities Within Confederation, as presented to the Royal Commission on Maritime Claims*, 21 July 1926.
33. Ibid.
34. Ibid.
35. Phyllis Blakely, *Glimpses of Halifax: 1867–1900* (Belleville: Mika Publishing, 1973), 13.

Chapter 3
1. House of Commons, "Halifax Winter Port," *Sessional Papers*, 1881; Tupper Papers, George P. Black to Sir Charles Tupper, Minister of Public Works, 20 January 1879.
23. Black to Tupper, 20 January 1879.
3. Macdonald Papers, Sir Hugh Allan to Sir Charles Tupper, 8 March 1880 and 15 March 1880.
4. Macdonald Papers, D. Pottinger to Collingwood Schreiber (chief engineer, Government Railways), 13 April 1880.
5. Macdonald Papers, George Taylor (general passenger and ticket agent, Moncton) to Sir Charles Tupper, March 23, 1880.
6. Macdonald Papers, F. Braun to Hugh and Andrew Allan, 1 December 1880.
7. Macdonald Papers, John Doull (president of the Halifax Chamber of Commerce) to Sir Charles Tupper, 19 November 1880.
8. Macdonald Papers, M. B. Daly to Sir Charles Tupper, 23 November 1880.
9. Macdonald Papers, H. and A. Allan to F. Braun, 11 December 1880; George Taylor to C. Schreiber, 15 December 1880; G. W. Robinson to George Taylor, 16 December 1880; George Taylor to C. Schreiber, 16 December 1880. The Central Vermont Railway was bought by the Grand Trunk in 1885; Allan was very close to the GTR's owners and may have been swayed by them. See Ken Cruickshank, *Close Ties: Railways, Government, and the Board of Railway Commissioners, 1851–1933* (Montreal and Kingston: McGill-Queen's, 1991).
10. Macdonald Papers, D. Pottinger to C. Schreiber, 13 December 1880.
11. Macdonald Papers, John Doull et al. to Sir Charles Tupper, 18 March 1880.
12. Macdonald Papers, L. E. Baker to John Doull, 10 March 1880. L. E. Baker of Yarmouth, a shipowner with one of the largest fleets in Nova Scotia, offered to carry grain from Halifax at sixpence per quarter less from Halifax than from New York on account of the shorter voyage required.
13. Cited in Eric Sager, *Maritime Capital* (Montreal and Kingston: McGill-Queen's University Press, 1990), 252; and Canada, House of Commons, *Sessional Papers*, 1881, ix. No. 61. Indeed, data furnished by the Board of Trade seems to bear out their assertion. Port costs for W. J. Stairs's *Esther Roy* were $2,368 in New York versus $1,498 in Halifax. Likewise, his *William Douglas* was $876 in New York versus $167 in Halifax, and his *W. J. Stairs* was $642 in New York compared with $150 in Halifax.
14. *Monetary Times*, 7 January 1881 and 18 February 1881. The memorialists included J. J. Bremner, T. E. Kenny, Isaac Mathers, W. J. Stairs, Michael Dwyer, and H. M. Doull. The cost of a grain elevator was estimated to be $100,000, for both the wharf and elevator.
15. Macdonald Papers, Collingwood Schreiber to F. Braun (secretary, railways and canals), 13 April 1880.
16. Ibid.
17. Ibid.
18. Halifax City Council, Minutes, 10 December 1880; Macdonald Papers, John A. Mackasey to Sir Charles Tupper, 21 January 1881.
19. Macdonald Papers, D. Pottinger to C. Schreiber, 13 January 1881.

20. Macdonald Papers, F. Braun to H. and A. Allan, 26 January 1881.
21. Macdonald Papers, H. and A. Allan to F. Braun, 28 January 1881.
22. "Haligonian," *Monetary Times*, 18 February 1881.
23. Ibid.
24. *Monetary Times*, 18 March 1881.
25. *Monetary Times*, 1 April 1881.
26. Thompson Papers, #000449, Stairs to Abbott, 31 October 1891.
27. Ibid.
28. Ibid.
29. Thompson Papers, #17166, Stairs to Thompson, 4 November 1891 and #17272, 16 November 1891.
30. Abbott Papers, Sir William Van Horne to J. J. C. Abbott, 10 November 1891.
31. Thompson Papers, #000554, Stairs to Abbott, 17 November 1891.
32. Ibid.
33. Macdonald Papers, #000552, J. F. Stairs to J. J. C. Abbott, 17 November 1891; Halifax *Herald*, 17 November 1891. Stairs learned of the new development as he penned his first letter, before the ink was even dry.
34. Thompson Papers, #17286, Stairs to Thompson, 18 November 1891.
35. Abbott Papers, Stairs to Abbott, 4 December 1891.
36. Thompson Papers, #18919, Stairs to Thompson, 8 April 1892 and #19421, 4 June 1892.
37. Jay White, "Conscripted City: Halifax and the Second World War," PhD thesis, (Hamilton: McMaster University, 1994) 9.
38. Ibid.
39. Blakeley, *Glimpses of Halifax*, 29.
40. Ibid.
41. Ibid., 40.
42. Raddall, *Warden of the North*, 233.
43. Canada, House of Commons, *Debates*, 18 August 1903; also quoted in "Railway Cut Development," www.halifaxurbangreenway.org.
44. Borden Papers, Borden to Laurier, 23 January 1911, NAC, MG 26, H, Vol. 132, p. 70008, reel C4353.
45. Halifax Board of Trade, *Annual Meeting*, 20 January 1914.
46. Department of Railways and Canals of Canada, *Report to Hon Frank Cochrane, Minister of Railways and Canals on Halifax Harbour* (1913), 31.
47. Ibid.
48. White, "Conscripted City," 40.
49. Ibid.

Chapter 4

1. Raddall, *Warden of the North*, 235. Based on the bank of Canada's inflation calculator, this total of $52 million would amount to almost $985 million in 2008.
2. M. Stuart Hunt, *Nova Scotia's Part in the Great War* (Halifax: Nova Scotia Veteran Publishing Co., 1920). This reference and the estimated total troop movements kindly provided by Dr. Jay White, e-mail Jay White to James Frost, 23 March 2006.
3. Raddall, *Warden of the North*, 241; see also Roger Sarty, *Canada and the Battle of the Atlantic* (Montreal: Art Global, 1998), 22.
4. Sarty, *Canada and the Battle of the Atlantic*.
5. Gurney Smith, *King's Yard*, 38
6. For the role of Sydney in the war see Brian D. Tennyson and Roger Sarty, *Guardian of the Gulf: Sydney, Cape Breton, and the Atlantic Wars* (Toronto: University of Toronto Press, 2000).
7. *Halifax, Canada's Atlantic Port*.
8. David B. Flemming, *Explosion in Halifax Harbour: The Illustrated Account of a Disaster that Shook the World* (Halifax: Formac Publishing, 2004), 20.
9. See Raddall, *Warden of the North*; Flemming, *Explosion in Halifax Harbour*; Hugh Maclennan, *Barometer Rising* (New York: Duell, Sloan and Pearce, 1941); Robert

McNeil, *Burden of Desire* (San Diego: Harcourt Brace, 1998); Janet Kitz, *Shattered City: The Halifax Explosion and the Road to Recovery* (Halifax: Nimbus Publishing, 1989); Alan Ruffman and Colin D. Howell, *Ground Zero: A Reassessment of the 1917 Explosion in Halifax Harbour* (Halifax: Nimbus Publishing, 2004); Laura MacDonald, *Curse of the Narrows: The Halifax Explosion 1917* (New York: HarperCollins, 2005).
10. Raddall, *Warden of the North*, 259.

Chapter 5
1. Ernest R. Forbes, *The Maritime Rights Movement* (Montreal and Kingston: McGill-Queen's University Press, 1979), viii.
2. *Report of the Royal Commission on Maritime Claims* (Ottawa: King's Printer, 1926), 21.
3. Ibid.
4. E. R. Forbes, "Misguided Symmetry: The Destruction of Regional Transportation Policy for the Maritimes," in E. R. Forbes, ed., *Challenging the Regional Stereotype: Essays on the 20th Century Maritimes* (Fredericton: Acadiensis Press, 1989), 114–135. See also Ken Cruickshank, "The Intercolonial Railway, Freight Rates and the Maritime Economy," in Kris Inwood, ed., *Farm, Factory and Fortune: New Studies in the Economic History of the Maritime Provinces* (Fredericton: Acadiensis Press, 1993), 171–196; E. R. Forbes, "The Intercolonial Railway and the Decline of the Maritimes Revisited," *Acadiensis*, Vol. XXIV, No. 1, Autumn 1994, 3–26; Ken Cruickshank, "With Apologies to James: A Response to E. R. Forbes," *Acadiensis*, Vol. XXIV, No. 1, Autumn 1994, 26–34.
5. HPA Archives, "Memoranda of Halifax Harbour Commission Prepared for Use of Sir Alexander Gibb," (1931), 26.
6. HPA Archives, Halifax Harbour Commission, "Brief Submitted to the Imperial Shipping Committee" (London, February 1929,), 9.
7. Sutherland, Fingard, and Guildford, *Halifax*, 140.
8. "Brief Submitted to the Imperial Shipping Committee," 14.
9. Sutherland, Fingard, and Guildford, *Halifax*, 145–146.
10. Felicity Hanington, *The Lady Boats: The Life and Times of Canada's West Indies Merchant Fleet* (Halifax: Canadian Marine Transportation Centre, 1980), 21.
11. Alexa Thompson and Debi van de Wiel, *Pier 21: An Illustrated History of Canada's Gateway* (Halifax: Nimbus Publishing, 2002), 31.
12. HPA Archives, HHC Box 2, HHC to P.J.A. Cardin (Minister of Marine and Fisheries), 26 February 1930.
13. This ship would later gain notoriety as the Jewish refugee ship that was refused entry to Havana and Miami in 1939 and forced to head back to Europe.
14. HPA Archives, HHC, Box 2, "Report to the Deputy Minister on Proposed Programme of Future Work at Halifax," 14 February 1930.
16. White, "Conscripted City," 55.
17. HHC Minutes, 16 October 1930.
18. Halifax Harbour Commissioners, *The Open Gateway*, Vol. 1, Nos. 1 and 2, February and March 1931.
19. HHC Minutes, 25 July 1931.
20. Sir Alexander Gibb, "Dominion of Canada, National Ports Survey, 1931–32, Report," (Ottawa: King's Printer, 1932), 122.
21. Ibid., 121.
22. White, "Conscripted City," 60.
23. Raddall, *Warden of the North*, 270.
24. White, "Conscripted City," 197.

Chapter 6
1. See White, "Conscripted City."
2. White, "Conscripted City," 7.
3. Marc Milner, *Battle of the Atlantic* (St. Catharines: Vanwell Publishing, 2003), 8.
4. Raddall, *Warden of the North*, 274.
5. Sarty, *Canada and the Battle of the Atlantic*, 135. Ultra intelligence was the anti-submarine code breaking

system developed at Bletchley Park in Britain, which was used to route the convoys.
6. Ibid., 158.
7. Ibid.
8. Victor L. Settle, "Halifax Shipyards, 1918–1978: An Historical Perspective," MA thesis (Halifax: Saint Mary's University, 1994).
9. The author's great-uncle, Myles Foster, was chief engineer on board the *St. Roch*. F. S. Farrar, *Arctic Assignment: The Story of the St. Roch* (Toronto: Macmillan of Canada, 1974).
10. See *Mission: North West Passage* (National Film Board of Canada, 1994).
11. White, "Conscripted City," 197.
12. Ibid., 202.
13. Ibid., 208.
14. Robert G. Halford, *The Unknown Navy: Canada's World War II Merchant Navy* (St. Catharines: Vanwell Publishing Limited, 1995), 242.
15. Ibid., ix. See also W. H. Mitchell and L. A. Sawyer, *The Oceans, the Forts, and the Parks* (Liverpool: Sea Breezes, 1966).
16. Halifax *Herald,* 20 November 2005, 3; Stephen Kimber, *Sailors, Slackers, and Blind Pigs* (Scarborough: Doubleday Canada, 2002).
17. R. E. Caldwell, "The VE Day Riots in Halifax," *The Northern Mariner*, Vol. X, no.1, 3–20.
18. Ibid., 4.
19. White, "Conscripted City," 386.

Chapter 7
1. HPA Archive, NHB Annual Reports, 1944, 1945, 1946.
2. W. D. March, *Red Line*, 339, quoted in White, "Conscripted City," 91.
3. Trudy Duivenvoorden Mitic and J. P. LeBlanc, *Pier 21: The Gateway that Changed Canada* (Hantsport: Lancelot Press, 1988), 131.
4. Hanington, *Lady Boats*, p. 126.
5. Ibid., 129.
6. Ibid.
7. Robert J. McCalla, *Water Transportation in Canada* (Halifax: Formac Publishing, 1994), 159.
9. See Shipping Conferences Exemption Act.
10. HPA Box 9, PQ 6, "Port Promotion."
11. Port tonnage was now expressed in metric tonnes as opposed to imperial tons.
12. According to a former clerk at the National Harbours Board in Halifax, the port's tonnage figures were exaggerated so as not to look so bad. This might explain the difference between perception and reality.
13. Ray March to G. P. M. Welch, 2 September 1966, HPA, Box 14, Port of Halifax Commission files.
14. Interview with J. W. E. Mingo, 7 December 2004.
15. R. March to Port of Halifax Commission, 12 December 1966, HPA, Box 15, Port of Halifax Commission files.
16. J. W. E. Mingo, speech, 11 October 1972, HPA archive.
17. Ibid.
18. Ibid.
19. J. E. Belliveau, S.D. Cameron, and M. Harrington, *Iceboats to Superferries: An Illustrated History of Marine Atlantic* (St. John's: Breakwater Books, 1992), 147; Vancouver Port Authority, "50 Years of Containerization," brochure and display, November 2005.
20. Peter Hunter, *The Magic Box: A History of Containerization* (Ottawa: ICCA Canada, 1993), 1.
21. Ibid., 67.
22. Interview with J. W. E. Mingo, 7 December 2004.
23. "Industry and Publicity," J. R. Mitchell to James O'Hagan, 23 November 1967, HPA, Box 1, Folder DE 18.
24. Interview with J. W. E. Mingo, 7 December 2004.
25. Hunter, *Magic Box*, 69.
26. Ibid., 52.

27. See Alexander C. Pathy, *Waterfront Blues: Labour Strife at the Port of Montreal, 1960–1978* (Toronto: University of Toronto Press, 2004).
28. Interview with the author, 28 February 2008.
29. Hunter, *Magic Box*, 70. Hunter is quoting from the Halifax *Mail Star*, 21 November 1970.
30. Ibid., 69.
31. Frank Broeze, "Containerization and Globalization of Liner Shipping," in David J. Starkey and Gelina Harlaftis, eds., *Global Markets: The Internationalization of the Sea Transport Industries Since 1850*, Research in Maritime History No. 14 (St. John's, 1998), 401–402.

Chapter 8
1. *Journal of Commerce*, 1 March 1996.
2. G. B. Norcliffe, "Industrial Development and Port Activity in Halifax-Dartmouth," *Canadian Public Policy*, Vol. VI, No. 3, Summer 1980.
3. Arthur D. Little Inc., "Feasibility of Developing a Transportation Gateway for North America at Halifax," Nova Scotia Department of Development, 1978.
4. DREE 1975 Subsidiary Agreement.
5. Arthur D. Little Incorporated, "Feasibility of Developing a Transportation Gateway for North America at Halifax," quoted in Norcliffe, "Industrial Development," 539.
6. Norcliffe, "Industrial Development," 540.
7. Testimony of Michael L. Sclar, NSARM, Halifax-Dartmouth Port Development Commission Records, NTA, c. N-17, RSC 1970, 10 November 1981.
8. McCalla, *Water Transportation in Canada*, 107–127.
9. Canadian Marine Transportation Centre and Dalhousie Centre for Development Projects, "The Economic Impact of the Port of Halifax," 1979.
10. Gardner Pinfold Consulting Economists Limited, "Port of Halifax Economic Impact Study," October 1991.
11. Halifax Port Authority, "Economic Impact Highlights," 1997.

Chapter 9
1. Halifax Port Authority, *Annual Report*, 1999, 2.
2. Halifax Gateway Council, "Economic Impact Study," InterVISTAS Consulting Inc., 2005.
3. Drewry Shipping Consultants, "Global Shipping Insight: Forward Thinking on the China Factor," July 2004.
4. Halifax Port Authority, 2005–06 advertisement.

Image Sources

The numbers following image sources represent the page numbers on which images from that source appear. T represents photos at the top of the page, M at the middle, B at the bottom, L on the left side, and R on the right side.

Appleton, Thomas E. *Ravenscrag: The Allan Royal Mail Line*: 46
Blupete.com: 9B
British and Colonial Press/Library and Archives Canada: 79
Climo: 97B, 100, 101T, 101B, 102, 108, 109, 114, 115B
Collections Canada: 9T
Dartmouth Heritage Museum: 23, 25
Deveau, Alan E.: 1, 5, 6, 199, 208T, 210, 211
Farmer, Steve: 70–71L, 73, 93, 167, 168, 169, 189, 190, 194, 195, 197, 198T, 198B, 200, 201, 205, 206, 207, 209
Fraser, Allen: 99, 105
Gauvin & Gentzel: 115T
Haliburton, Thomas Chandler. *History of Nova Scotia*: 22
Halifax Port Authority Archives: 63, 69, 77, 95, 98, 103, 104, 106L, 106R, 143, 145, 146, 147, 151, 152, 155, 156, 157, 184, 186, 204, 208B
James, Albert: 172
Mariners' Museum, Newport News, VA: 29

Nova Scotia Archives and Records Management: 2, 8, 10, 12, 14L, 14R–15, 16, 18, 20, 21, 24T, 24B, 26, 27L, 27R, 32, 33, 34, 35, 40T, 40B, 41, 42, 43, 47, 48, 49, 50, 51, 52–53, 54, 56, 57, 64, 65, 66, 67, 68, 71R, 72, 74, 75T, 75M, 75B, 76, 78, 80, 81T, 81BL, 85, 86, 87, 89, 90, 96, 97T, 110, 111, 116, 117, 126, 133, 134, 138, 141, 163, 192
Parker, Mike. *Running the Gauntlet*: 121
Parks Canada: 81BR, 82, 83, 88, 119, 120, 122T, 122B, 123, 124, 125T, 125B, 130T, 130B, 131, 132
Pier 21, Canada's Immigration Museum: 135, 136, 137, 193T, 193B
Public Archives of Nova Scotia: 36, 128, 129
U.S. Historical Archive: 31
Wamboldt-Waterfield Photography: 150, 159, 160, 161
WHW Architects: 202T, 202B
Wright, Ken/Sundancer Photo Communications: 173, 174, 183, 187, 188T, 188B
Zeidler Partnership, Architects: 203T, 203B

Index

A

Acadia Sugar Refinery 71, 77, 83, 110
Age of Sail 1, 31–32
Allan, Hugh 30, 46, 50, 52, 56
Allan Line 30, 46, 48, 50, 52, 56, 59–64, 68
Aquitania 137, 138
Athenia 120
Atlantic Container Line (ACL) 159, 161, 167, 179
Autoport 180, 182, 184

B

Banks, Hal 139
Battle of the Atlantic 119–25, 130–31. *See also* Second World War
Beck, Ray x, 142, 174
Bellefontaine, David 174, 193
Bennett, Richard B. 103, 117
Borden, Robert L. 67, 68, 78, 79, 88
Boston, Port of 177, 196
Britannia 28–29, 30, 200
British Navigation Acts 18, 19

C

Canada Marine Act 191, 193
Canada Ports Corporation 174, 192. *See also* National Harbours Board (NHB)
Canadian Government Railways (CGR) 90
Canadian National (CN) 5, 97, 155, 173
Canadian National Railways (CNR) 90, 92, 94, 107, 151, 153
Canadian National Steamships (CNS) 97, 118, 131, 139, 140, 142
Canadian National Steamships labour dispute 139
Canadian Northern Railway 90
Canadian Pacific Railway (CPR) 3, 60, 61, 90, 94, 104, 112, 173, 181
Canadian Pacific Ships (CP Ships) 171, 176, 181
Canadian Seamen's Union (CSU) 139, 140
cargo-handling 125, 127–30
Cartier, Georges Etienne 41
CAST 171, 173, 181
Ceres Incorporated 174, 210
Champlain, Samuel de 7, 8
Chesapeake 13, 14

China Effect 194
Civil War (U.S.) 1, 37–41
Clarke Traffic Services 155, 158
Clarke Transportation Canada Ltd. 5
Collins, Enos 16
Confederation (Canadian) 3, 41–42, 45, 50, 54, 55, 58, 105
Consolidated FastFrate 6, 207, 208
containerization 151, 158–59, 162, 165, 166–68, 176–179, 180
convoys 80, 82, 119, 120–23, 125, 129, 218
Cornwallis, Edward 8, 9
Corsair 21, 22
Cowie, Frederick 69, 71–72, 110
Cowie Report 69, 71–73
cruise industry 198–99
Cunard Centre 6, 191, 201
Cunard Line 24, 27–28, 30, 44, 60, 62, 68, 118, 200
Cunard, Samuel 21, 24, 26–28, 30, 34, 200, 201

D

d'Anville, Duc 8
Dart Containerline 5, 155, 156, 158, 161, 171, 173
Deep Water Terminals: activity at, 3, 77, 80, 107, 113; construction of, 63, 64, 77, 94; photos of, 64, 77, 78; problems with, 69; proposed expansion of and improvements to, 71, 108; transfer to HHC of, 93
Depression. *See* Great Depression
Dominion Coal Company 88, 90
Dominion Line 62, 63, 64
dry dock (Halifax) 77, 94, 123
Duncan, Andrew Rae 92, 97
Duncan Commission 92, 94, 107

E

European and North American Railway (E&NA) 37

F

Fairview Cove Container Terminal 6, 173, 174, 179, 190, 196, 210
fast line issue 45, 59–63
First World War 4, 77, 78–82, 90, 120
Flemming, Jock 41

G

gateway initiative 168, 170–171
Gibb, Alexander 105, 107, 110, 112–113
Gibb Report 105, 107, 110, 112–113
grain elevators 4, 54, 55–56, 58, 64, 186–187
grain handling 52, 54, 55, 58, 108, 143, 147, 185–187
Grand Trunk Railway (GTR) 3
Great Depression 91, 101, 104–5
Greenbank 71, 150, 152

H

Halicon. *See* Halifax International Containers Limited
Halifax and Liverpool Trading Company. *See* Halifax Packet Company
Halifax Board of Trade 62, 67, 68, 105
Halifax Dockyard 63, 79, 83, 87, 88, 110, 113, 123, 124
Halifax Explosion 4, 78, 83–88
Halifax Farmers' Market 6, 202
Halifax Gateway Council 194
Halifax Harbour Commission (HHC) 92–95, 97, 101, 102, 103–105, 107, 114, 192
Halifax International Containers Limited (Halicon) 5, 156, 173
Halifax, Liverpool & London Steamship Company 63
Halifax Packet Company 21
Halifax Port Authority (HPA) 192, 193–195, 196, 201
Halifax Port Commission 149, 150, 153, 175
Halifax Port Company 130
Halifax Port Corporation (HPC) 174, 175

Halifax Seaport 202
Halterm Container Terminal 5, 6, 154–57, 159, 161–62, 163, 175, 191, 208, 210
Hapag-Lloyd 161, 167
Hetherington, J. L. 103, 104
Hope, James 40
Howe, C. D. 127
Howe, Joseph 34, 35–36
Huskisson, William 17

I

immigration 137–138
Imo 83, 84, 87
Imperoyal 71, 88, 94, 104, 110
Intercolonial Railway (ICR): as a conveyor of goods from Halifax to inland markets, 41, 42, 45, 50, 52, 54–56, 58; freight rates on, 48, 90, 92; freight volumes on, 56, 63; government support of, 48, 50, 54–55, 58, 112; incorporation into Canadian National Railways, 90; incorporation of European and North American Railway into, 37; inefficient routing of, 3, 58, 107; proposed extension of, 46
International Longshoremen's Association (ILA) 127, 158, 177–78

K

Kauffeld Report 153–54
Kauffeld, Theodore J. 153
Kawasaki Kisen Kaisha Line ("K" Line) 175, 180, 190. *See also* Tricon
Kneiling, John 153–54

L

labour disputes. *See* Canadian National Steamships labour dispute

Lady Boats 97, 99, 139, 140, 142. *See also* names of specific boats
Lady Drake 97, 99
Lady Hawkins 97, 99
Lady Nelson 97, 99
Lady Rodney 97, 139, 140. *See also* Lady Boats
Lady Somers 97
Laurier, Wilfrid 67, 78
Liverpool Packet 14, 16
Liverpool, Port of 27, 71
Los Angeles–Long Beach, Port of 181, 195

M

Macdonald, John A. 41, 42, 54
MacDonald, Vince 128, 129
Mackenzie King, William Lyon 88, 103
Maersk Line 175, 176, 181, 190
Manchester Liners 5, 171
March, Ray 149, 150
Maritime Rights Movement 91, 92
Mauger, Joshua 9
mercantilism 17
merchant mariners 130–31
Mingo, J. W. E. (Bill) x, 149, 150–51, 155
Missions to Seamen 131–32, 178
Mission to Seafarers. *See* Missions to Seamen
Monbeton de Brouillan, Jacques-Francois de 7, 8
Mont Blanc 83, 84, 87
Montreal, Port of: berthing space at, 117; CAST and, 173; container terminal in, 5, 154, 162, 176; disadvantages of location of, 71; expansion of, 196; grain handling at, 107, 186; St. Lawrence Seaway and, 4, 144; traffic levels at, 137, 143, 171, 177, 181, 182, 196; wartime convoys and, 82; winter accessibility of, 3, 5, 144, 148

N

Napoleonic Wars 11, 13
National Harbours Board (NHB) 113, 144, 150, 151, 155, 174, 192
Naval Yard (Halifax) 32
Neptune Orient Line (NOL) 175, 180, 190. *See also* Tricon
New York, Port of 71, 158, 177, 182, 196, 207
Niobe 78, 79
Norfolk, Port of 177, 182, 196
Nova Scotia College of Art and Design (NSCAD) University Port Campus 6, 202

O

Ocean Terminals: construction of, 4, 73, 76, 88, 90, 117, 142; maps depicting, 63, 69, 70; photos of, 68, 71–76, 81, 89, 96, 114, 138, 141, 143, 147, 188; proposals for, 69, 71–73, 101, 110, 113; traffic at, 107; transfer to HHC of, 93
Oldfield, Karen vii–viii, ix, 194, 211
Olympic 79, 80, 81
Orient Overseas Container Line (OOCL) 175, 180, 190, 195, 204, 207, 208. *See also* Tricon

P

Phinney, E. C. 103, 104
Pier 21, Canada's Immigration Museum 6, 191, 193
Pier 21 (immigration shed) 4, 101, 135, 137–38
Plant Line 64, 67
Port Development Commission 193
Portland, Port of 3, 62
Public Cold Storage Terminals Ltd. 4, 94–95, 97, 143, 147

Q

Quebec City, Port of 71, 82, 162, 176, 177, 186
Queen Mary 2 198, 200

R

Reciprocity Treaty of 1854 37, 38
Report on the Affairs of British North America 34
Richmond Terminals 3, 4, 69, 77, 87, 93, 94, 117, 187, 188
Royal Canadian Navy (RCN) 119, 123
Royal Commission on Maritime Claims. *See* Duncan Commission
Royal William 27, 28

S

Saint John, Port of: berthing space at, 117; containerization at, 162, 165, 176–77; as Halifax's rival for trade, 17, 20, 37, 90, 117, 165; photo of, 18; rail service to, 3, 90; traffic levels at, 137, 148, 196; wartime convoys and, 82
Seafarer's International Union (SIU) 139, 140, 142
Seawall Defence 147
Seaward Defence 150
Second World War 4, 99, 119–25. *See also* Battle of the Atlantic
Shannon 13, 14
Shubenacadie Canal 21–25, 26
Smart Port 194
Stairs, John F. 59–63
Stairs, William 21, 22
St. Andrews and Quebec Railway (SA&Q) 36
St. John's, Port of 20
St. Lawrence Coordinated Service 171, 173
St. Lawrence River 148–49
St. Lawrence Seaway 4, 5, 143–44, 149, 154, 187
string strategy 180–81
St. Roch 124–25

T

Tallahassee 39–41
Thompson, John S. D. 59, 62
Treaty of Aix-la-Chappelle 8
Treaty of Utrecht 8
Tricon 175, 176, 180–81, 190. *See also* Orient Overseas Container Line (OOCL); Neptune Orient Line (NOL); Kawasaki Kisen Kaisha Line ("K" Line)

U

unions. *See* Canadian National Steamships labour dispute; Canadian Seamen's Union (CSU); International Longshoremen's Association (ILA)

V

Vancouver, Port of 162, 176, 181–82
Victory in Europe Day 132–34

W

War of 1812 1, 13, 16, 22
Wentworth, John 21
Wier, Benjamin 38–39
winter port issue 3, 45–46, 48, 50, 55, 56, 58, 59, 61, 68
World War One. *See* First World War
World War Two. *See* Second World War

Z

Zim Container Service 161